From Bounced Checks to Private Jets

THE MASTERY OF MIRACLES

Hazel Ortega

Acknowledgements

To my siblings Claudia, Rosie, Jeanette, Brenda, Adrian and Jesse, thank you for being the best part of this journey. I dedicate this book to all of you. Los quiero mucho!

This book is an anthem for those who are struggling!

My darling Frances, you are my North Star. I was lost until the day you were born. As you grew, so did I. Being your mother is the best thing I've ever done. You will always be my baby even when I am old. I feel so proud you are a part of me.

Thank you to my parents who are in heaven. You taught me many lessons but most importantly, you showed me unconditional love. To my uncles Carlos, Armando, Tony and Ruben, you were each important father figures to me when there was no one there. Tia Martha, you are like a second mother to me. Thank you for always being there for us no matter what. Judge Barbara Burke, you became a mentor and showed me the value of finishing my high school education. To Edward R. Ortega, my first Latino role model, thank you for seeing potential in me that I could not see in myself. Thank you to my mother-in-law Graciela, without your love and tender care for my daughter, I could not have made it through school. To my business coach, Marianne Emma Jeff, who showed me how to upgrade my vision and run a million dollar plus business that allows me use my passion and experience to help others. Lastly, to all the rest of my family and close friends, you mean the world to me.

My dearest Elbert, thank you for making me laugh. Life is better with you.

Table of Contents

Part 3: Mastering Your Miracles

The Phone Call: October 1994

My phone rang and jolted me out of a sound sleep. Blurry-eyed, I looked at my clock. 1:00 AM. By then I knew that good news never comes from a call in the middle of the night. Steeling my nerves, I reached for the phone and answered.

"Hello?"

"Hazel," came my mom's panicked voice, "You need to come and get me."

"What? What's happening?" I asked confused.

"Come and pick me up! Right now!" she cried urgently.

There was a terror in her voice that I didn't question. I sat bolt upright in bed.

"Lo mate. I killed him."

I threw on some clothes and sped to meet her.

Introduction: There is No Quit in Me!

By the time I was born on December 3rd, 1971, my mom and dad were separated. I had pneumonia when I was born. As a newborn I had to be put into an ice bed to get my fever down. My mom reached out to my dad at that time because she was scared for me. She thought I would die because I was so sick. This brought them back together. I was their miracle baby.

When I finally got better and was allowed to leave the hospital I was two weeks old. My parents took me straight from the hospital to a park to drink and party with my dad's friends. It was December, so it was cold out, even for Los Angeles. My parents wrapped me in a jacket and left me in the back seat of the car.

When it got even chillier outside, one of my dad's friends came back to the car to get his jacket. Not realizing that I was inside, he pulled his jacket off of the backseat, and I came flying out of it. With some bumps and bruises, they took me right back to the hospital, and I was admitted again. My mom was really pissed off at my dad, and my dad beat up the guy who accidentally tossed me out of his jacket. My dad said for years he would randomly punch that guy and say, "This is for what you did to my daughter."

And that is how my life began. My young parents were still a bit wild and obviously they didn't know a lot about parenting. This chaos foreshadowed what was to come.

When you know your personal story is one that will make heads snap up, jaws drop, and invite a LOT of shock and sympathy, it begins to feel like a sort of accomplishment in itself. *Look what I've been through. It happened to me, and I survived it. This is who I am.* It's like a badge that you wear with everything. I'm sure at some level I must have known that there was much more to me than what happened around me and where I came from, but when you live and breathe your story it can become your mark. Even if you don't share your story with a lot of people, it shows. You give off the "I've been through some shit" vibe. It fuels your fire, but simultaneously keeps you from healing and growing.

When you become "stuck in your story" it becomes nearly impossible to see things from any other perspective. The view is blocked by the pain and rejection you've experienced. You know the details so intimately that they affect every step in your day. When you repeatedly tell yourself that you have been abandoned and thrown away, or that no one cares about you, all you will see around you are things that prove this to be true. You will be unable to see any other outcome, even if it is right in front of you.

Why did I believe that my story was so much worse than yours, or anyone else's? Why did it define me for so long? I grew up in a rough area where most people were dealing with the same issues that seem to plague low income neighborhoods--drugs, gangs, death, and crime. What right did I have to feel like the bigger victim? I played that part for a long time, *the victim*. But what I have come to realize is that there is no *quit* in me.

Chapter 1: There's Always a Story Worse Than Yours

"If we all threw our problems into a pile and saw everyone else's, we'd grab ours back." - Regina Brett

In 2006 I had just finished my Master's Degree and I was starting my job as a psychologist. I thought I was doing pretty well in the world, but my then-boyfriend told me that I was not loving. I wasn't affectionate. I didn't say the words he wanted to hear, and I didn't demonstrate my feelings for him. I thought that my feelings were implied by the simple fact that I was *with* him. I didn't know how to speak the language he craved. I had a hard time showing love even with my mom and sisters. I didn't grow up with hugs and cuddling. It just wasn't like that with us.

I didn't resent him for this though. He was a good man and very patient with me and my issues. I understood his need for a more loving partner and I wanted to find out if I had that kind of affection and demonstrative love inside me. Years before this, a friend had told me about a personal development seminar she had attended that had helped her get beyond some of her issues. I had also met a man who was running for public office just after he had made a speech to a huge crowd of people. I asked him how he was able to talk so comfortably in front a group. He told me he had attended the same seminar. He said, "If you do it, you're not gonna be afraid to talk in front of anybody. You could talk to the President of the United States." That sounded like a miracle to me. I was sold.

I found the phone number for the program and registered right away. They were about to jump into a sales pitch and I cut them off. I said, "I don't need that. I'm ready." I had already done the research. I was committed.

The seminar was held at a hotel conference space in Los Angeles near the airport and would run for three days. They were long days, as the program was from 9:00 a.m. to 10:00 p.m. I got up earlier than usual because it was completely across town. I took time off work and arranged for extended childcare for my three kids. Most conference attendees stayed at the hotel, but I went back and forth to be with my kids and because the cost of childcare and a hotel stay was too much for me.

On the first day, I arrived a little bit late. I thought it was no big deal. I got there at 9:15 and sat down. The woman running the program very pointedly said that if we weren't going to take the program seriously, we should leave. Even though I had arrived with a few other late people, I could feel that she was talking to me. I felt terrible. This just increased my commitment. I was all in.

The heads of the program would propose ideas and people in the audience would raise their hands to disagree or ask clarifying questions, and then they would be asked to come up to the microphone at the front of the room. People were invited to share their stories.

We were asked to talk about the stories we had created. It didn't make sense. People were getting up and saying, "I didn't create a story. This is what *happened to me*." I wasn't buying into the whole idea that we created our stories either. It was basically a long parade of people getting up and objecting, saying, "That's great, but it isn't true in my case. I'm different." I was sitting there the whole time thinking, "Yeah, that's right. I'm different too."

They were trying to make us see that the content of our stories is not who we are. However, we often let the content become our identity. Little by little, some of what the leaders were saying made sense, but I still listened to all of these peoples' stories and in the back of my mind there was a little voice saying, "Yes, that's true for them. They are creating *their* stories, but none of these stories are worse than mine." I had a good one.

I had been sitting there for about four hours when I heard a story that stopped that voice in my head. A young woman, about 27-years old confidently walked up to the microphone. She began to talk about how her older sisters did not love her. They did not call her, ask about her, or look for her when she had been out of touch for a while. When she was a kid, they would slam their bedroom doors in her face.

Then she moved on with her story. She had a different father than her sisters. When she was just a toddler, her father molested her 13-year old sister and got her pregnant. Even when her mother found out, she did not leave him.

Soon after, at a family party, she was playing with her father, sitting in his lap when one of her cousins, enraged about the molestation, shot and killed him. She said his blood was all over her. She was only three years old when it happened. She was extremely emotional, sobbing, and she went into great detail about it. I felt as if I was standing right there in that living room with her.

It was a horrendous, shocking story. I think that is the worst thing that can happen, your father being killed right in front of you as a child. It was so sad. It made me think that compared to hers, my story was nothing.

In that moment, the myth that my story was different was completely busted. I thought that I had this untouchable story and there were so many reasons for people to feel sorry for me. That day I saw an opening where I could change things for myself. Up until that moment, I had been using my story as proof of why my life wasn't working, even though I had already been making changes in my life. Against the odds, I had just completed a hard-earned Master's degree and was just starting my work as a psychologist. But I came from living in a poor neighborhood where drive-by shootings were commonplace. I had family members who had been killed in these shootings. Even with the education and becoming a professional, there was still all of this old drama and pain inside of me.

After I heard this young woman's tragic story at the conference, I really understood how we create and add bullshit to the stories of our lives. We contribute so much unsubstantiated detail without any proof--just letting our insecurities and suspicious minds run amok. To her story, the young woman had added her feeling that her sisters didn't love her. In her mind, the proof was that they slammed their doors in her face when they were younger. The presenter said, "Well, ask the audience how many teenagers out there want their three-year-old, five-year-old, or seven-year-old sister coming to their door when they're sharing secrets and being teenagers? Nobody wants a little kid in the room." Then he asked all the whole group how many of us kicked our little siblings out of the room when we were growing up. Of course everybody raised their hands. She was building the evidence in her own mind and using it to feed the belief that her sisters did not love her.

The presenter challenged her by saying, "I want you to call your sisters now and find out if they love you." She was adamant that they would not answer their phones. They would be too busy. They never answered her calls. The speaker urged her again, "Promise me you're going to go right now, go to the hall and call your sisters." After a break, she returned and shared that she had called her sisters. They did accept her call and through tears they told her how much they loved her and that they thought that she was the one who had been aloof with the family. They thought she didn't want anything to do with them.

It was an entirely different reality that she couldn't see previously. She had presumed that she was hated by her family. She didn't dare to ask that terrifying question: *Do you love me?* But once she had spoken with her sisters, she couldn't deny the answer. The love was there. All those walls and stories she had created crumbled with that truth.

When I witnessed this, I knew that my story--*all of my stories--* were holding me back. My family drama, the accolades I got from people for raising my brothers, my ability to get an education despite my poor upbringing, my mother being in jail; I was attached to it like a lifeline. I got a lot of pity and attention for having a sob story. It was like I was trying to see how much burden I could take on to prove my worth. It was a kind of martyrdom.

This realization was the first in a long line of miracles to come. I wasn't willing to let my story restrain me anymore. It was time for a serious plot twist. I could do better and I deserved better. My story would be one of my choosing. My past would be not my excuse, it would be my incentive for rising.

Chapter 2: Broke, Not Broken

"The poor are an especially important resource for innovation when they have the bravery and pluck to get out of the poor places in which they're living." - P. J. O'Rourke

I was born in General Hospital, East Los Angeles, California. I was raised in downtown L.A. where all the high rises are now. Most of the places where my friends and I played around as kids are big corporate buildings now. Before the high rises were built, my neighborhood was small houses and big, battered apartment buildings, many liquor stores and small markets. It was a poor and very dangerous neighborhood. I lived in a big low-income apartment building with about 60 apartment units.

I grew up near Echo Park in Los Angeles. That 20-block neighborhood was the whole world to me then. Echo Park had been a home to gangs since the 1970's. They were part of the makeup of the community. The real gangsters were violent; fighting and killing other gang members. By the time I was nine years old, there were probably ten different rival gangs in my neighborhood. In the exact corners of my area, we were "protected" by the gang "Eighteenth Street." "Diamond Street" was their biggest adversary. If you lived in one of their territories, you were considered under that gang's protection. You had to be careful if you crossed into another territory.

My mom married and divorced many times. We moved from different apartments with each different husband, but always within the same building. It was almost comical. I lived in that building from the ages of one year to nineteen years old. I think we must have moved at least 10 times. It was always an apartment with one bedroom and one bathroom for the seven of us. The five girls slept in the living room and my mom and whichever husband would be in the bedroom. Most of the apartments in our building had lots of people crowded into them. There were cockroaches everywhere. Everywhere. Everywhere! Rats too sometimes. My mom had a cockroach go into her ear once. She could feel it wiggling inside her ear. She had to go to the hospital to have it removed. This was not uncommon but it freaked us all out.

Because everyone around us lived in similar situations, I didn't know that I was poor. I didn't know any different, I just knew my mom never had money. She was always borrowing five dollars from people here and there. Sometimes it was money for us to ride the bus or to buy food. She would borrow two eggs from a neighbor so we had food. She always owed people money. We were on welfare, so we would get some government assistance, but we were forever scraping by.

I remember when our iron broke and my mom just cut off the cord and we would turn on the stove and use the heat along with the broken iron to press our clothes. We used the oven to dry out our tennis shoes after we washed them in the sink. When I was in middle school I walked four miles to and from school when there was no money for the bus or if I had spent it on a snack instead.

There was about a month when we didn't have gas to heat our apartment. We had to go to our neighbors' apartments to heat food or take showers. When neighbors wouldn't let us shower there, we used buckets of cold water to bathe. Let me tell you, cold water showers are just miserable.

My mom worked off and on as a waitress and went to school for a time. Out of nowhere she married this guy named Juan who she met in a bar. She only knew him for about four days and she brought him home to live with us because she was tired of her current husband cheating and lying to her. Overnight Juan became our step dad for the next nine years. She didn't love him. She said she just needed a home for us and he paid all the bills.

During those nine years, she did not work. Juan would give her 300 dollars a month and she made miracles happen with it. She went to second hand stores and garage sales to buy used things and resell them at a higher price. She was a business woman. She would set up a blanket at the park or in front of our building and then sell stuff there. She sold things we had around the house. She took my things or my sister's things to sell. She sold everything. I always thought if I wasn't watching out, she would sell the shoes off of my feet.

In high school, we were all starting to get excited about the prom. I knew I wanted to make it a special night, but when it came to paying for my prom dress, I was on my own. My best friend, Patty, and I took two weeks off school and got minimum wage temp jobs at a clothing store called The Broadway (it's Macy's now). We had to catch a bus at 5:30 in the morning to get to the warehouse and they worked us hard. I worked for two long weeks tagging clothing with a tagging gun, and constantly poking my own fingers with it.

Patty and I would talk while we were working and the manager, Mrs. Bowman would scold and separate us. I remember one day she threatened me, "If you want to continue to work here and have a job, you need to shape up or you're going to get fired. You're going to lose your job." She was horribly rude. I remember thinking to myself, "Yeah right, lady, this is not where I'm going to work for long. I am only here for my prom dress. I only have two days left here." But then I realized that there were people working there who had to stay to make their living. People couldn't just skip out when they'd made enough money. Mrs. Bowman was nasty to everyone and they just had to take it.

When the two weeks were over, I had earned 200 dollars to buy my prom dress, a white French lace gown that made me feel like a princess. My mom and my sister helped me with jewelry and the cost of my prom ticket. Everyone pitched in what they could so I could have that beautiful prom night I had dreamed about. I was thrilled.

My date was also my first boyfriend, a white boy named Gabriel. The fact that he was white was the only reason my mom let me date him. My sister, best friend, and I, along with our dates rented a limousine to drive us to the dance together. When we walked into the prom, I was amazed at how beautiful everyone looked. It was magical. It was as if I was a completely different person. I felt like Cinderella risen from the ashes of my real life and entering a royal ball. I had rarely even owned new clothes before and here I was in this lovely, creamy, lace dress. It was the happiest day of my life and I never wanted it to end. Unlike Cinderella, my mom allowed us to stay out all night so the group rented a hotel room to keep the celebration going when the prom ended. The next morning, I came home and immediately sank into bed, exhausted, happy, and still wearing my prom dress. I slept hard and gradually faded back into real life. The Cinderella dream disappeared like smoke in the air.

One week later, without asking me, my mom took my cherished prom dress and sold it for 15 dollars.

Chapter 3: Life and Death in Echo Park

"No kid is seeking anything when he joins a gang; he's always fleeing something. He's not being pulled; he's being pushed by the circumstances in which he finds himself." - Greg Boyle

Many of my school friends had trendy clothes and things that I couldn't afford. Hello Kitty stuff was really trendy when I was in junior high school. I finally got this Hello Kitty bag and I loaned it to a friend. We had a fight and "broke up" as friends and she refused to return it, so we got into a fist fight.

I shoplifted a lot. I always seemed to be stealing. I saw what other people had that we didn't. We never had "extras" like craft supplies at home, so I would take things. Even in elementary school when I was very young, maybe 6 years old, I took things from school. I took glue, construction paper, scissors, erasers, and pencils and hid them away in a closet. When I got older I mostly stole jewelry and accessories from thrift stores. I would just carefully put things in my purse when nobody was around. When my purse was full, I would give it all away to my friends. I gave the cool girls the jewelry to kind of "buy" their friendships because I felt like I was lacking in so many other areas. My mom wouldn't let me wear jewelry at that age anyway. If she saw me with something like that, she would ask me where it came from and find out the truth. She was really good at catching me in lies so I could never let her see it.

I suppose stealing didn't seem like such a big deal to me compared to the other crimes that were constantly going on in my neighborhood. It started with the football teams. We were all associated with the football teams from our schools. The other teams were our adversaries. In the beginning it was a rather friendly competition, but then the real gangs started backing up different teams. They were easy to spot because the guys in my neighborhood were usually preppy types. The gang members were Cholo types with baggy pants, white T-shirts, and tattoos. They added to their gang by recruiting members from our football teams.

I was nine the first time I feared for my life. I was playing with a bunch of other kids on the patio in front of our building. Some of the kids were younger than me, some were older. A car came screeching up with a bunch of guys yelling their gang name, and all of us just scattered. Everyone was running. Older kids trampled over younger kids to get away. It was absolute chaos. People ran into different apartment buildings, and into other people's private apartments, including mine. I had been knocked down in all the panic, so I got up as quickly as I could and ran toward my own apartment. There were people I didn't recognize running in and out of the doors, and when I got inside my own place, there was a guy hiding in our hallway. My mom saw him and rushed him out right away. I sat at the window and watched the rival gang members drive away. It was over, but I knew I had been in danger.

I saw this time and time again as a kid. Gang members from other areas would often drive up in front of our building, get out, and start a fist fight with guys from my neighborhood. Sometimes they fought with knives too. When it was over, they would get back in the car and drive off.

As I grew older and more accustomed to seeing gangs as part of my daily life, they started looking more interesting to me. They looked cool. Part of the appeal was the protection. At school everyone knew where you lived, so you were associated with a gang no matter what because of your neighborhood. I have a cousin who lived in Diamond Street territory which was the arch enemy of 18th Street. We would only speak to each other in the bathroom at school, because we could not be seen together in public. She lived in the other territory, so that was just how it was for us. All of this created a lot of tension at school, and a lot of fights, but there was a sort of coolness to it.

I had known my friend David Alejandro since elementary school. He was a really likable guy and we always had such a good time together, laughing and playing around. We played a lot of dodgeball together. He liked hanging out at my building because older gang guys hung out there. He was 13 years old and wanted to get their attention and get involved with them. Like I said, we all thought they were cool. His gang name was "Wabbit," like "rabbit" with a "W," but I never called him that.

One day David and I were waiting at the bus stop with a bunch of other kids heading home after school. The tension was higher than usual that day. There were members of multiple gangs there together and a fight broke out. Of course we all ran, as usual. This was friction we saw and felt every day and sometimes things turned out OK. But the next day it came out that after the rest of us had run off, David had been stabbed and killed with an ice pick in the fight.

Everybody was talking about it. We all knew what had happened that day, but what stands out to me now is that we all just moved on afterward. Of course I was incredulous about it when it first happened. It hit me how someone could be with you one day and dead the next. But there wasn't much room for emotion. We had so much pressure and stress in our daily lives that we just went on. We acted like it was normal. No one asked us how we felt about it. No one explained what had happened. David was just gone. This 13-year-old kid we all knew had been murdered in public and life carried on.

Soon after that one of the neighbors I grew up with was arrested for killing another gang member. He had tortured him, repeatedly running him over with his car, back and forth. Then after he ran him over, the rumor was that he cut his penis off. He went to jail, which was the first time I started to see how scary this life was. I saw consequences and it just kept getting worse. I didn't think it was cool anymore.

Not long after that the drive-by shootings started. Several times a month gang members would open fire from the windows of a slow moving car and speed off once their clips were spent. They could flee the area before the police were able to get there. Our building got shot up a lot. The people who lived on the first floor were in constant fear. We lived on the second floor, so sometimes we didn't even know about it until morning when we saw the bullet holes everywhere. It was terrorizing. Sometimes I knew the people who had been in the car.

Three of the older boys in my neighborhood were on the run after committing a drive-by one night and while they were driving away the police started chasing them. Someone must have reported them. When the chase got intense, my friends' car went over the side of an overpass in downtown L.A. They lost control of their convertible Mustang and it flipped, killing two boys and leaving one in critical condition. One way or another, that way of life was costing lives.

When I was about 11 years old we heard there was going to be a fight between the 18th Street gang and MS-13, or Mara Salvatrucha, a Salvadorian gang. It was like an organized event. The whole neighborhood knew it was happening and they were excited about it! Everyone was all amped up. It was like 18th

Street was our sports team and we were going to cheer them on. My mom even took me to watch the fight.

It was about 5pm and still light out. It was a very hot and sticky day; the kind of heat that feels oppressive even though I was wearing shorts. The crowd was buzzing with excitement. This was our neighborhood standing up for itself. We were going to show everyone that they couldn't mess with us. My mom was pumping her fist up in the air and yelling, "Andale!" *Go for it!* We were standing with our gang and letting them know that we were behind them. Chants of "Chingatelos!" (meaning "Fuck them up!") were drumming through my ears.

Because the other gang was Salvadorian, this was really a cultural battle. Mexicans generally looked down on them. Now I see that we just didn't know each other. We were so busy judging each other that we couldn't get along. Growing up poor means always being in protection mode and looking for danger. Anything different from what you know feels dangerous.

My mom and I hung back just a little. We walked with the crowd behind "our" gang of about 50 guys as they moved in for the fight. When our gang rounded a street corner we couldn't see what they saw, but suddenly they had done an about face and were charging back in our direction. Then we saw. The Salvadorian gang was twice as large as ours and they were coming at our guys with machetes in the air. It was mind-blowing. It looked like something out of a war movie or Game of Thrones. They appeared as savages to us, truly horrifying.

My mom grabbed me and we flew down the street. I don't think my feet even touched the ground. It was a scene of sheer pandemonium and lawlessness with everybody running in different directions to disperse and get out of the way. We were in the middle of a modern-day war. I was terror-stricken.

After that day, my mom became more protective of me and my sisters. She had always been scared of the neighborhood, but as we grew older and the area became more dangerous, she knew we had to be careful. We weren't supposed to talk to the boys or spend time with them. If it looked like we were veering into that lifestyle, she would put a stop to it.

One time I made a fake tattoo on my hand with a marker. It was three dots which is a common prison tattoo that means "mi vida loca," or "my crazy life." (I've since learned that it is also said to represent what gang life leads to: 1. the grave 2. the hospital 3. prison.) When my mom saw this she smacked me.

We made these keychains in class that we would put gang names on and girls would hang them on their purses. My mom wasn't having any of that. I wasn't allowed to wear black because that's what the Cholas wore. I wanted the high hair and the thin eyebrows, but she wouldn't let me have them. I wasn't allowed to wear makeup. She didn't want us to dress like them or talk like them. We couldn't cuss. We couldn't say the word "stupid." Nothing like that.

A lot of my family lived near us in Echo Park. Some of them lived in our same building. My Aunt Isabel and cousins, Dora and David lived across the patio from us. We were like siblings. David was only six months older than me and we did everything together. We ate at each other's' homes several days a week. We went to school together every day. When we were older, I set him up with my friends.

Music and dance were really big with me and David. Rap, breakdancing--all of it. We memorized all of the words to "I Need Love" by L.L. Cool J. We'd record the song off of the radio and then start and stop the tape so we could write down all of the lyrics and learn it by heart. We were experts at performing that song. We thought we were awesome.

One night when I was 20 years old I was on the phone with my sister, Claudia, and she told me that she had heard through the neighborhood that our cousin David had been shot. We were trying to figure out what had happened when I heard a loud knocking out in the hallway. There's something about a police knock that is distinctive, and I knew it well by that age. I got off the phone and got the detective's attention. He asked me if I knew who lived in apartment 3 and could I see if they were home.

I checked my aunt's door and it was unlocked. I looked inside, but there was no one there. I went back to the police and let them know that the apartment was empty.

"Miss, do you know David Lepe?" the detective asked.

"Yeah, he's my cousin."

"Okay, he is dead and I need to talk to his parents."

"He's not dead," I replied.

"Yes, he is."

"No. *He is not*," I insisted.

The detective glanced at the officer next to him and a bit impatiently said again, "Yes, ma'am, *he is*. He is deceased. He is dead."

He showed me David's driver's license. "This is him, right?"

I couldn't respond. Shock overtook me and I screamed, "What? No! No!"

"Ma'am, he is dead. Here is my card. Have his mother or father give me a call," he said matter-of-factly. Then they turned and walked out.

David was actually amongst those who had initiated a drive-by. He was in his car with three friends, one of whom was a marine and completely unrelated to the gang, but who went along with his friends anyway. David turned off the headlights and turned the corner onto the target street, then sped down the street while the back seat passengers pulled out their guns and began shouting their gang name and shooting out the window. Because there were many drive-bys in the gang neighborhood, we don't know if they were tipped off or they were just always ready for deadly encounters but they managed to shoot back at my cousin's speeding Mustang hitting him in the neck. He crashed his car soon after and everyone jumped out of the car to run for their lives while the gangsters were chasing and shooting at them.

My cousin David Lepe was a smart, funny, loving, 21-year-old who was ironically training to be a police officer while running around with gang members from our neighborhood. And now he was dead too.

When shock turned to anger, my sister and I wanted some kind of revenge and vindication for David. We wanted to know who had killed him. We wanted them to hurt like we hurt. We even devised a plan to find the killer, seduce him and then take him somewhere and kill him ourselves. We wanted to inflict pain and suffering--to run him through with a knife and leave him to die alone. We really thought we would get away with that. We didn't seek to bring a stop to the craziness, because that didn't happen where we came from. We brought in more anger and aggression. That is the way it was. If someone was killed in one gang, there was retaliation--no question.

The shock of that night had to wear off eventually, but the terror never wore off. We were surrounded with death; surrounded by fear and chaos. Our circumstances threatened to swallow us up daily. When the phone rang in the middle of the night, we couldn't assume it was just a wrong number or a friend who had run out of gas needing help. We came to always expect horrible, violent news. To this day, a phone ringing in the night jolts me. I instantly think it's something awful. I think if I saw a cop at my front door, I'd faint. When my brothers go out to a club or go hang out in the park I worry and feel like they could die. I literally have a feeling that they could die. It's a form of PTSD. It has never gone away.

Chapter 4: Life Lessons from "The Bradys"

"If you know what you did was wrong, that's more important than any punishment." - Carol Brady, *The Brady Bunch*

It became pretty easy for me to get away with misbehaving because my mom didn't speak or read English. If a note came home from school I would just tell her what I wanted her to know and that would be it. She would never know if I got into trouble. In junior high school I got suspended for tagging one of our neighborhood gang signs on the floor of a classroom at school. We were having a Christmas gift exchange and the kid I was gifting to asked for spray paint. My mom had to buy it for me, but then the kid didn't show up at school on the day of the exchange and I just thought, what the hell?

I had done graffiti before--even in the hallways of my own apartment building! I'd also cross out other gang tags. The assistant principal caught me tagging at school and I was put into a group of "graffiti busters" where I had to clean up graffiti around town. I just told my mom I was volunteering.

On this day in junior high school the other kids stood in a circle around me so I couldn't be seen. We had a substitute teacher that day and that poor woman had no idea what was going on, she could barely deal with the class anyway. So I took my white spray paint and made a huge, sprawling "RSL" on the floor.

Of course I got caught. The sound and the smell of spray paint are hard to miss. When I had to tell my mom about the suspension I changed the story and said that I had written my name on the floor. I told her it was very small and that the school was making a big deal out of it. She was still furious. Even though she had no idea that I had written something gang-related, she said it was the dumbest thing I could have done. If she had only known.

I created my own gang nickname, Cuddles. I wasn't actually *allowed* to have a gang nickname, but Cuddles sounds nice and my mom thought it was cute. When I think about it now, she must have known it was a gang name. Everybody in the neighborhood had a nickname to go by, which was better than your real name, because it was covert. Your teachers didn't know, your parents didn't know, and it was cool. Like a code name. Only badasses had nicknames, like alter egos. There was Boppy, Wabbit, Chino, Magic, Bird, my best friend was Snuggles and my older sister was Baby Freak. My little sisters were known as Pebbles and Babs.

When I was in 9th grade we all went to a ditching party, where you skip school and have a daytime party. When we got there the house was packed with kids by 10:00 A.M. The radio was on and people were talking so it was really loud. It was a tiny little house so 50 kids made it really difficult to move around.

The sound of gunshots cut through the roar of the crowd and the music. We all recognized the sound of a drive-by and everyone in this tight crowd panicked and tried to scatter. We trampled over each other. It was a terrible commotion, with people bumping into each other and trying to get out. There were probably 25 people in front of me trying to get out the back door. I made my way to the kitchen and jumped out of the window and ran. There was a guy on crutches with a cast on his leg and he jumped out too, crutches and all. That's just what you do during a drive-by, you drop or you get out and run. No one was hurt at the party, but it was another terrifying reminder of the clear and present danger of the lives we were living.

Sometimes my mom would be driving us somewhere and when we drove through certain parts of the neighborhood, I would hang my hand out of the car window and make the hand sign for RSL. My mom never knew about it, but I was representing my neighborhood. I thought I was really cool, like *we rule.*

That's the thing about my mom; she didn't participate much in what we did. She didn't value school activities or sports. Not knowing much English, she couldn't read to us when we were young and she couldn't help us with our homework. In fact, she never cared to look at our report cards except to see our attendance records to make sure we were not ditching school. This was true for a lot of the adults around us. She was with us almost all the time, trying to protect us. She was adamant that we stay away from gang life, but she didn't offer an alternative to move our focus elsewhere. Our entertainment was TV, radio, and especially the drama created within the gangs. There was a ton of *chisme,* or gossip. When I was part of that life I felt popular and wanted. There was a seduction and an exhilaration that came from doing something fun/dangerous and I got swept up into that. I didn't question it. I didn't know anyone who lived outside of our neighborhood. *It was the only reality.*

Every so often I would ditch school to get out of my neighborhood. The feeling that gave me, just a small, temporary escape felt like absolute freedom. It was like going to another country. I would go to the beach or to the mall--the usual teenager hangouts--and I saw that not everyone lived the way we did. These tiny tastes of freedom were hard to return from, but I knew I had to go back. That 10 mile stretch of Echo Park was my entire life and I didn't know the way out yet. I didn't even know I wanted out yet.

My other entertainment/escape was television. From the ages of four to nine, I was home with my siblings watching TV pretty much all the time. This was a period when my mom was working and going to school. We were left alone and forbidden to leave the apartment. She left us alone all day. My sister, Claudia and I looked after our four-year-old twin sisters. We woke in the morning so we could tune in to watch other people living false lives. We'd get up around six in the morning and turn on the TV and stare at it until my mom came home in the evening and we were allowed to go outside.

That TV was our babysitter. It entertained us and taught us life lessons. It took over our lives. We loved *The Brady Bunch*, *Three's Company*, *The Addams Family*, all of those shows. The TV molded me. *The Brady Bunch* showed us that no one likes a tattletale. I would repeat that lesson to my sisters so they wouldn't tell my mom about some little thing I'd done wrong. *No tattletales.* In a way, I'm grateful for the exposure to all of those shows. They usually wrapped up with some kind of moral which bridged a gap between what we were taught by my mother and what we were learning on our own.

TV was the window through which we could see another world. This is how I came to understand that we were poor. We could never have the things the people on TV had. The characters on TV were rich, white people. I didn't see people on TV that looked like us or lived like us. We weren't represented at all. The white people on TV weren't working at the gas station to make rent while self-medicating with cigarettes and drugs. They were business men and comfortable housewives in large homes, with happy children. That wasn't us. That was just the truth of it.

Chapter 5: My Sisters, My Mother, and Her Lovers

"Children learn what they live." - Dorothy Law Nolte

I'm the second of seven children. When my mother became pregnant with my older sister, her boyfriend left her. Before her pregnancy was showing, she met my father and he wanted to be with her and be the baby's father. He told my mother, "You could say I'm the father of the baby. It'll be our secret, we won't tell anybody." They stayed together through her pregnancy and everyone believed he was the father. But when my sister was born, it was clear that he was not. She didn't look like him, she didn't look like my mom. She had the exact features of her biological father who was dark-skinned and had very distinct facial features. There was no denying her paternity, it was written all over her face. People began to talk and my mom worried that she would end up alone, so she wanted to get pregnant again to keep her man around. She was sure that he would leave otherwise, knowing that the baby wasn't his and that everyone could see it.

I was born 11 months later. My mom got pregnant during the 30 days after my sister was born so that my dad would stay. My dad was 18 years old when I was born, and he was a gang member. All of his friends were gang members. He and my mom had their own apartment and the gang members would hang around our place. My dad was always cheating on her. He would come home with hickeys and girls would pick him up at the house. My mom told me that he was drinking and doing drugs during that time.

One day when my mom was still pregnant with me, she was driving with my aunt Martha and she saw my dad in a car with a girl. She stopped the car and got out to confront my dad, hitting the girl in the car. My dad stormed out of the car began to hit my mom. He kicked her in the mouth. My mom had really weak teeth due to malnourishment from growing up poor in Tijuana. He knocked out her four front teeth with that kick. She was all beat up. My dad beat her up.

My parents had no idea what they were doing. My mom told me that my dad would smoke weed around me when I was a baby. He was in and out of jail because he stole cars and other petty crimes. They would go to the market together and take me in my stroller so they could steal food and baby formula. They would hide it in the stroller, in my diaper, or in their clothes. My mom went on welfare. My dad brought home jewelry and things that he stole from other gang members. He never worked a regular job. He knew how to take parts off the body of a car, so he would steal cars and then sell them off in parts. For years I thought he was an auto body mechanic.

Even though my dad cheated on my mom a lot, he finally said, "I'm going to marry her." The day they got married, they were supposed to attend a party to celebrate afterward. My mom took my dad aside after the ceremony and told him, "Huero, I'm not going with you to the party. I only married you because you said you'd *never* marry me. Now that we're married, I've gotten what I wanted, but I don't want to be with you anymore." That day my mom left him, and she was never with him again. The *day* of their wedding. My aunt told me from then on she saw my dad getting into harder drugs and more serious crimes. He was doing heroin and participating in armed robberies.

After that, my dad wasn't really a part of my life anymore. He would go to jail for several months, then five years, then seven years. He was just in and out all the time. He would write to me from jail and every time he got out he would come and look for me. His letters included his release date and that would be the day he would come to see me. We always lived in the same building so I was easy to find, even after several years. All of my life he had that pattern. I think he missed me while he was in jail. He had little bouts of freedom when we would see each other, and then he'd be gone again.

When I was two years old my mom moved in with a new boyfriend, Cuco, who would become the father of my two sisters, the twins, Jeanette and Rosie. From the beginning, the twins were very different from one another. Everything about Jeanette is amplified. She is a minute younger than Rosie, but Rosie was quite a bit smaller when she was born so she came out first. Jeanette's eyes are larger, her voice is loud and she is a big personality. Rosie is very soft-spoken and she is finer-built. We used to call her "Gatita" which is "kitten" in Spanish. Rosita Gatita.

Cuco and my mom fought all the time. One time I caught him forcing himself on my babysitter. I don't think he was raping her, but he was trying to make out with her and he was definitely aggressive. She was a young girl screaming for help, so I went into the kitchen and I got a fork, and I stabbed at his back with it. He wasn't wearing a shirt, but it still really didn't hurt him. I was just so little. I was maybe three or four, I don't know. But he was as close to a father as I had. I loved him like he was my dad, there was no distinction. I didn't really want to hurt him, because I'd learned to love him like a father, but I did want to help this screaming girl. He finally pushed himself up and left the room in a huff. The babysitter gathered up her things, and hurried out in silence.

My mom knew what had happened with the babysitter and with me trying to stab Cuco, but that didn't end their relationship. They had other problems, he also had an expensive cocaine habit and many more fights ensued. He would leave for days at a time and come back and they'd start at it all over again. One time he left for his birthday and my mom said, "If he leaves and he doesn't come back home tonight then he can't live here anymore." From what I remember, he left for his birthday and stayed away for the entire weekend. That was when my mom brought Juan to live with us. She had been scoping out other men and when Cuco stayed away too long, she moved him out and moved Juan in. When my stepfather finally came home, he knocked on the door, and Juan answered and told Cuco, "You don't live here anymore. This is my house now." My mom had already packed all his things and dropped them at his sister's place. My step dad was like, "Fuck you, this is my house, these are my kids." Juan, who was still a stranger to us kids, told him, "No, this is my family now. You don't live here anymore."

Naturally this lead to a fist fight, and the police came. It was really awful; we could hear everything. All of us kids were in the house, screaming, "Oh my God, what's going on?" Then my mom closed the door and left us inside while she dealt with the police. Anyway, from that moment forward, he never came back for me and my older sister. He would come back just to see the twins, but not us.

On the weekends we'd hear my mom say, "You're going with your dad today," so all of us would rush to get ready but it was only the twins he wanted. He was a jeweler and he would give them gifts like gold necklaces, and would bring nothing for Claudia or me. I just didn't understand. He had been our father too for all that time, and now we were like nothing to him. When he came into the building we would run for him and my mom would stop us and say, "No, not you." His sister also lived in our building and when he came to visit her, Jeanette and Rosie would go see him but we were not allowed. It was so odd because we called his sister our aunt, she was our tia, but when he was around we weren't welcome. It was all so confusing.

Ultimately, the twins lost their dad too. He met a woman and moved away to Texas with her. They only saw their dad a handful of times after that. None of us had our fathers in our lives growing up.

As it turned out, the experience with our mom's new guy, Juan was horrendous. We missed our dad, Cuco and saw Juan as the reason we couldn't be with him so we hated him. In the end, I realized Juan provided much needed security in our lives; I now appreciate him for giving me the most stable years of my young life. However at the time we didn't even know this guy, and he was *our father* now? We were actually supposed to think of him that way, as our father. My mom just met this guy over the weekend and suddenly he's supposed to be "Dad."

Most of all he was *not our dad.* He was a stranger, and he was not nice to us. I felt that he took all of our mother's attention. I hated him for that. He tried to step in and discipline us. We would fight amongst ourselves a lot. We fought over things like food, because there was never enough. A little thing like a danish would become a big deal if one of us got it and the other didn't. My mom, sisters, and I were all the same size, so we constantly fought over clothes. Honestly, we would fight over anything. A full-on, screaming argument could break out over whether Boy George was better than Michael Jackson.

We were loud, like most kids are. My mom especially wanted us quiet at the dinner table, but we weren't. How are you going to keep four kids quiet? It's impossible. So she would yell and hit us. Juan actually fought with my mom over that, telling her not to hit us. But once my sister, Claudia, disrespected him somehow, and he spanked her and he hit her across the face with a belt.

He didn't speak English, and he had a lot of issues. He drank too much and he was very argumentative. My mom didn't love him, so they would fight, and he would say, "Rosa, why don't you love me? You're my wife!" She really didn't even like him all that much. Having a man was just so important to her, so he was better than nothing for a time. I wanted Cuco to come back and I thought if Juan left, he could be with us again.

Juan watched TV in the living room, which was our bedroom, our space. We wanted to go to sleep and we couldn't because he'd have that damn TV on. We had no privacy and nowhere else to go. We were young ladies and we had no place that was ours. I remember when I got my menstrual cycle, I was so embarrassed about it. I had to get my Kotex, and all of my stuff was in the living room with my clothes. There he sat, just staring at the TV while I tried to sneak what I needed out without being obvious. I did *not* want him to see. I was so shy. Even if a commercial came on television about Kotex when he was there, I'd be so frickin' embarrassed. My sisters and I couldn't have conversations because he was always in our space. He didn't understand. He would bust in on our conversations. I couldn't be on the telephone with my friends because the telephone was in the living room and he was always right there. He was just annoying. Then he would drink and go out, and my mom would get mad about that.

Then my youngest sister, Brenda, arrived 5 years later. She was so cute and we loved her a lot but it was left up to my sisters and me to take care of her. I began to resent her. My mom and her husband didn't have enough money to go out and take all of us so they would just take her. I saw a divide happening. They used to buy her these little danishes as treats and bring home one bag of Cheetos and say it was only for her. I hated her for that. Of course it wasn't her fault but I hated her because they treated her different. You know, we all wanted treats. Of course we did. My mom didn't seem to realize how unfair this was to the rest of us. As usual, there was not enough money. Brenda's dad wanted to give her special things because she was his only child. *Not us, her.*

My mom would leave for long days, and Brenda would be left with us. Many times, mom and her husband would go out together and leave her with us, and she would cry and cry. I remember yelling at that poor baby, "Shut up! Shut up!" I felt bad about it as I was saying it, but I just didn't know how to calm her. Even when my mom was home, if Baby Brenda was crying, she expected us to take care of her. We had no idea what we were doing! We didn't know what babies needed. I told her, "You're the mother. Take care of your own daughter."

If Brenda ever fell or hurt herself, we were to blame. I remember my older sister being smacked around by my mom when Brenda took a tumble one day. "That's not *her* daughter!" I screamed at my mother. I had been mopping the floor and suddenly she turned on me. The floor was wet all over and she just started hitting me. I slid all over the place and she picked me up and threw me around. I actually slipped into the splits. She beat the hell out of me. It didn't matter what I said though. No matter how much I talked back to my mom and told her she was wrong, the responsibility of her 5th child fell to us.

It was such a stressful time. I wasn't equipped for caring for a baby. I didn't know what she needed. I would try anything to keep Brenda calm and quiet. We weren't allowed to leave the apartment, so I would take her into the closet. We had spiders:

daddy-long-legs. I would take Brenda into the closet when she was crying, and I would show her the daddy-long-legs. She didn't know what she was looking at and she was very entertained by it. I would also find cockroaches and cover them with a glass, and that would be her toy. She was totally amazed. We didn't have toys, so we used what we had. Sometimes we'd create little skits for her to watch. We'd pretend we were in gangs and "fight." My cousin David would come over and be the referee. I would say I was from Rockwood, and Claudia would say she was from the Rascals, another gang in our area. When we had enough we'd say "Mercy," and the fight would stop. David said he wanted us to know how to fight, so that if we did ever get into a real fight on the street, we would know what to do.

Juan stayed until I was 16. One day he was just gone. My mom told me he went to jail for a DUI. What I found out years later, though, is that he left her for another woman. That was really hard on her. I think maybe she did start to love him over the years. He had a new wife and he totally disappeared. This is when my mom started going out and partying a lot. She became very skinny and my Uncle Tony told me that she was doing cocaine. We were still young, and we needed her, but she told us, "From this point forward, all of you guys have to take care of your damn selves, because I'm going to take care of myself. All my life I've taken care of other people, now I'm going to take care of myself." True to her word, she stopped cooking and cleaning and would not wash our clothes any more. She had never really cooked for us much anyway. Our meals consisted mostly of malt-o-meal, mayonnaise and mustard sandwiches, tortillas with sour cream, cans of Campbell's soup, ramen noodles, and cereal for dinner. Sometimes we would get burgers and fries from the local diner. Everything we ate was processed and cheap.

Every so often my mom would promise to bring us food when she came home from work or partying, or whatever she had been up to. We went to bed hungry and she came home around two or three in the morning with food for us. She brought us Tommy burgers or sometimes McDonald's food or 7-Eleven hot dogs.

When my mom went out, she left four-year-old Brenda with us. Mom was working at a bar and would stay out all night, neglecting us, and then sleep through the next day. One night, Claudia snuck out of the house to meet friends and party, and when my mom caught her, she decided to move out. Claudia couldn't deal with my mother's wrath; the hitting and yelling. She was done. She had a job and some money, so she moved in with a friend. My mom was really upset about that, and even more resolute that she wouldn't care for us any longer. She said, "Everybody who I love leaves me, so you guys have to take care of yourselves." She was miserable and her drinking increased. She went out even more often.

One time, she knocked on our apartment door and I couldn't tell who it was. I asked over and over, "Who is it?" but I could barely hear her. She said "It's me, open the door." When I opened the door, she was on the floor and all bloody. She was out drinking and driving. She crashed into a tree near our apartment and smashed her face on the dashboard.   She looked like a monster. I called 9-1-1 even though she asked me not to. I heard her tell the police she had fallen.

Soon after, she began to date a neighborhood drug addict nick-named E.T. and she moved him into the apartment. He was also a dealer and would ride around on a bicycle, selling. I was always challenging her about how she was living her life, and telling her to be a mom and stop screwing around. My sisters, the twins were in an upward-bound program at school. They were cheerleaders too. They were doing remarkably well for themselves, despite the fact that my mom wouldn't come to the games where they cheered, or even drive them there. I would tell her, "But you're their mom. You're supposed to take them to the practices and support them." She would say, "No, if they want to be cheerleaders they have to take care of themselves. They have to figure it out."

My constant question to her was, "You're going out *again*?" I was in her face a lot. That was the reason she finally kicked me out.

The morning it happened my sisters were supposed to go away for a weekend with their upward-bound program to Occidental College. My mom was sleepy that morning, as usual, and the twins were frantically begging her to get up.

"Mom, you've got to take us to the bus stop so we can go to Occidental. This is a big opportunity for us!"

"Leave me alone," grumbled my mother from her bed.

Jeanette and Rosie came to me crying. "Hazel, mom doesn't want to take us, and we're going to miss the bus, and we're not going to be able to go for the weekend."

I was fed up. I stomped over to her bed and yelled, "Get up! Get up! Take your kids to the bus! That's what's important, not you partying all night long and having your boyfriends!"

Quick as a cat, she shot up and she grabbed me by my blouse with one hand. With the other hand she grabbed a plastic laundry basket, dumped the dirty clothes out of it and dragged me to the closet. (I had been so happy to finally have my own room--the closet.)

"You have one minute to grab as much as you can and put it into this laundry basket. Then you are out," she hissed viciously.

I was stalling, but she was hitting me the whole time. I didn't see what else I could do, so I started grabbing my stuff off the hangers and putting it into the laundry basket. Everything I owned fit into that laundry basket. I left nothing behind.

Then she grabbed me again and pulled me all the way down to the bottom of the stairs by my blouse. She opened the door and she told me to get out. When I didn't move she literally kicked my ass out the door, and she slammed and locked it. That was it, I was out of the house. My mom was free from the torture of my pleas and demands for her to behave like a real mother.

Chapter 6: On My Own and Still Cleaning Up Her Mess

"In search of my mother's garden, I found my own." - Alice Walker

I sank to the sidewalk in front of the building and cried, not knowing what to do or where to go. I was 19 years old. I had a job, but I didn't have any money saved. People kept passing by me and seeing my tears, but I was too upset to care. My Uncle Tony was passing by and stopped in front of me.

"Why are you crying?" he asked.

Through sobs, I told him what had happened.

"Fuck that bitch." Thinking for a second he said, "Good! Why are you crying? You have a job."

"Yeah, but I have no money," I choked, "I don't even have a quarter for the newspaper."

What my uncle said next changed my life forever. He put his hand in his pocket and he gave me a quarter, and he asked me, "Okay, what's your next problem?"

"I don't know where I'm going to go."

"Don't you have any friends you could stay with? I see you with a lot of girls all the time. You have friends. Think of who you could stay with."

My mind began to turn a bit. "My friend Maria, I could stay with her."

"Okay, call her."

We went to the phone booth and when I called Maria she said that I could go to her house. Her mom agreed that I could live there with them. I would share a room with Maria and her baby. It was very kind of them, but after two nights I realized it was too scary for me there. There was a drive-by shooting and I just couldn't stay.

It may seem odd that this would affect me so much, when I had seen plenty of drive-bys in my lifetime. The difference was that this wasn't *my* neighborhood. I didn't know the gangs in that area. More importantly, they didn't know me.

Uncle Tony came with me to look at apartments and we found a studio for only $375 a month, which included utilities. I went to my boss and asked for an advance on my paycheck, so that I could pay my first month and the deposit. I was lucky enough for him to agree. This was my very first job. I worked for a lawyer who practiced Worker's Compensation law and he gave me enough to start my life outside of my mother's home. Soon after, I got a credit card in the mail with a $500 credit line, so I bought furniture. After two weeks I had my own fully-furnished apartment with brand new appliances and everything I needed.

Later, my mom would say that she kicked me out because I went out to clubs with my friends and that I was a bad influence on my sisters. She tried to rewrite history, but I know that she just couldn't take my confrontations anymore. When things started to work out for me in my own place, she accused me of planning the whole thing myself. She didn't speak to me for six months and my sisters weren't allowed to speak to me either.

What saved me was that question, "What's your next problem?" I had been in shock and with that question I was able to move out of self-pity and to start solving my problem. I will always be grateful to my uncle for that question and the outlook it gave me. He taught me that life comes with problems and he showed me how to problem solve! We need to address them as they come.

Eventually, my mom came around and we began to mend our relationship. I tried to help her. I would give her $30 out of my paycheck every week. Then that wasn't enough and she wanted more. When I was doing OK financially, I bought her a car so she could get around more easily. Three days later she traded it in for a cheaper car so she could keep the difference in cash. The day I got my income tax return she came to my office.

"Hazel, let's go to the check cashing place down the street."

"We could, but those places take a lot of money to cash checks," I protested.

But she needed the money NOW, so we took the check into one of those places that will give you a payday loan and cash checks in exchange for a big fee for the service. They charged me $300 dollars of my $2,500 check. If I took the check to my regular bank, there wouldn't have been a fee at all, but they would probably have placed a hold on it for a day or two. It wasn't soon enough for my mom. Never enough, never soon enough.

I didn't ask her where the money went, but I had a pretty good idea. The money I gave her weekly seemed to help her, but she was always showing up for more money from me. Every time I got paid she was there waiting for the money.

When I was 22 years old, I found out she was pregnant again. This time it was by her boyfriend, Eddie. No one liked Eddie. He was also a known drug and gun dealer and he was a really mean guy. My mother was in her 40's and she devoted all of her attention to Eddie, doing cocaine with him and neglecting my sisters who were still in her care. When she got pregnant she decided to move in with him.

My sister, Brenda begged me to take her in. She was nine years old and would stay with me from time to time. She hated Eddie and my apartment offered a place without fights, drugs, and drama. My mom asked if Brenda could live with me and I agreed.

My brother, Adrian was born in 1993. The living situation with my mom and Eddie got predictably worse. Their fights increased and became violent. He hit her over the head with a guitar once and left a five-inch gash on her head. An ambulance came and she had to get stitches. Because he sold guns, he always had them around. He would regularly shoot at her feet during fights.

The drugs made it even worse. They were both oblivious to how toxic their lives were. Eddie cheated on my mom repeatedly and she really rolled with the drama of that. She began to neglect my baby brother. I was already caring for my sister Brenda, and then she began to leave the baby with me too. She went out to bars to try to chase down Eddie.

One night I was taking care of all of my younger siblings at my apartment and around midnight the police came to my door. My mother was in the back seat of their cruiser.

"Miss, do you know Rosa?"

"Yes. She is my mother." Panic was setting in.

They explained, she was driving erratically and the police turned their lights on her. She made a U-turn and made them chase her. Then she suddenly stopped the car and got out, running in high heels to escape them. They caught her.

"So miss, what should we do? Should we take her to jail, or should we leave her with you?"

Without skipping a beat, I said, "Take her to jail."

But the police wanted to give her a break. They felt bad for her and just wanted to scare her.

One of the cops winked at me and said, "I'm not going to take her to jail. I'm going to scare her. Go along with it."

"No," I said. "Take her to jail. Teach her a lesson. She's a bad mother. She has all of her kids right here in this apartment, I'm taking care of everybody. Not her, me!"

He went to my mother and said, "Rosa, you're going to jail tonight." My mom was crying, and yelling about what a mean person I was. She said she'd never forgive me.

"It's your fault, mom. You're the one who is getting into trouble."

The cop drove her around while lecturing her in an attempt to throw a scare into her. Then he dropped her back to my apartment, but she didn't come in. She went straight back to the apartment she shared with Eddie.

I had lunch with my mom and Eddie one day and at one point in the conversation he said, "If something was to happen to your mom, let's just say she would die for some reason, Adrian is going to come and live with me. That's my son. I will take care of Adrian."

I was taking care of Adrian a lot at this time and Eddie must have seen me as a threat.

"But my mom is young. There's no reason she wouldn't be around," I said, trying to play it off as fear was building inside by his insinuation.

"That may be true," he said menacingly, "but things happen, and if that day ever comes, I am coming for my son. That's *my* son."

This would come to be a familiar threat from him. *My son. My son. My son.*

More than one time, Eddie came to my apartment looking for my mom. When he was told that she wasn't there, he pushed his way in and searched every room, even the closets. Once he busted in as my sister Jeanette was getting out of the shower and he demanded that she get out so he could check for my mother in the bathroom. She wouldn't budge so he grabbed her arm and tried to move her out of the way. In the chaos her towel slipped to the floor and she stood there, naked and screaming at him to get out. He looked truly shocked and didn't move until my sister started throwing things at him as she screamed. He finally ran out and my sister called the police and they filed a report.

As with the men before him, the drama was never-ending in the relationship between my mom and Eddie. It seemed more and more possible that he would actually kill her. He once told me that he could kill her and take the baby to Mexico and live freely. He said that to my face.

Chapter 7: Waking Nightmares

"There are wounds that never show on the body that are deeper and more hurtful than anything that bleeds." - Laurell K. Hamilton

One night in October 1994, my phone rang and jolted me out of a sound sleep. Blurry-eyed, I looked at my alarm clock. 1:00 AM. By then I knew that good news never comes from a call in the middle of the night. Steeling my nerves, I reached for the phone and answered.

"Hello?"

"Hazel," came my mom's panicked voice, "You need to come and get me."

"What? What's happening?" I asked confused.

"Come and pick me up! Right now!" she cried urgently.

There was a note of frenzy in her voice that I didn't question. I sat bolt upright in bed.

"Lo mate. I killed him."

I threw on some clothes and sped to meet her.

When I pulled up I saw the curtains in the window move. She had been watching for me. I waited for her to come out, looking in all directions around me, terrified for her. Had someone reported a gunshot? Were the police on their way? What would Eddie's family do when they found out? What kind of revenge would they come for? Oddly, my own safety didn't cross my mind. I just wanted my mom to be safe.

I saw the front door open and my mom rushed out to me, in one hand she carried a knapsack and in the other she had my baby brother wrapped in a dirty white polyester blanket. She was wearing blue baggy pants and a grey zippered sweater. She flung the car door open, quickly got in and crouched down in the seat.

"Drive me to Tijuana. I'm going to stay with family. Money. I'm going to need money. First let's go to the bank and get some money."

"Mom, what happened? Are you OK?"

"I had to do it, Hazel! He was coming at me like the devil! The gun was right there and I grabbed it and he dared me to use it. He was going to...He would have..." her words seemed to elude her. "He was going to kill me."

"What did you do with the gun?"

"It is right here," she said, pointing to her knapsack.

"Mom! You have to get rid of it! We can't drive around with a gun!"

I pulled over and she threw the gun into a sewer. She got back in the car and said, "Now the bank."

My head was swimming. I knew she was telling the truth. He would have killed her. I just never imagined that she would kill him. It was almost like I was watching a movie of the two of us. It didn't feel real. What were we doing? Where was I driving?

"Hazel! The bank!" she insisted.

I snapped back to what I was doing. At the time I didn't have much money myself, so I did something crazy. I deposited an empty envelope into the bank's ATM. The machine allowed me to immediately withdraw my "deposit" as cash. I had $300 for my mother to use to run for her life.

Once she had her money, I started thinking. It was a two and a half hour drive to Tijuana. I could get into a lot of trouble for helping her leave the country. I needed to know what happened. This was dangerous. No one was on the streets but I felt like I was being followed the whole time. It was nerve racking. I could feel my knees shaking as I drove. We didn't have a car seat for the baby so my mom was holding my brother. We drove in silence for a long time and then she let out a deep sigh and told me her story.

"We were arguing. He was coming at me and he was going to hit me, so I grabbed one of his guns and I pointed it at him. Then he told me, 'Now you'd better use it. If you're going to pick it up, now you'd better use it.' He lunged at me and grew big and threatening. He was angrier than I have ever seen him! His eyes bulged and he looked at me ice cold. He flexed his muscles, ready to hit me. I was just trying to scare him! I just wanted him to leave me alone, but I woke up the devil with that gun. He lunged at me and I shot him."

My mother went on to tell me that she unloaded the gun into Eddie's chest. He fell and she just kept on shooting. She was so scared that he would kill her or the baby. Then her mind started racing and in her distress she desperately searched his things for money. She turned out his pockets, looked in his boots and there was nothing! Eddie always had money, but today, not a cent. She rummaged through his things, all the while petrified that he would rise up and kill her.

I stopped the car.

"Mom, I can't take you out of the country. We should go to the police. He threatened you all the time. He hurt you. You had to defend yourself!"

"No! I'm leaving. You have to get me out!"

"Mom, if I get caught, who will take care of the kids? I can't do it. We can't both be gone!"

"I'm *not* going to the police, Hazel. You don't have to take me, but I am going to Tijuana."

"But mom..." I stammered.

"No," she said emphatically. "No."

And with that, she opened the car door and jumped out. I was stunned as I watched her disappear into the night with my small brother in her arms. How would she get to Mexico? What might she have to do to get there?

Still dazed, I turned and drove straight home, scared, exhausted, and oddly relieved. The realization hit me that with Eddie dead, I didn't have to carry the fear of him killing my mother and kidnapping my brother anymore. I still feared for what would happen to my mother and Adrian as they ran off to Tijuana, but not having to fret about Eddie anymore gave me a huge feeling of relief.

Once I got home, I collapsed into bed. Just a few days later, I was startled out of sleep by the pounding on my door in the morning. I got up and went into the kitchen and suddenly there was a gun at my head.

"Put your hands up! Put your hands up!" an officer ordered.

"Who else is in the house?"

"My sisters are here," I said. They rounded up my sisters. The whole house was surrounded by police. The street was lined with patrol cars. They thought my mom was in the house.

They took all of us out of the house in our pajamas with our hands up, and they checked the entire house. They checked the neighbor's house too. We were handcuffed with guns pointed at us. Then they took us downtown to the Los Angeles Police Department, Rampart Division to interview us. My siblings and I had all agreed on a false story to tell the police. We practiced it together. Everybody stuck to the story, but when I was caught in a lie, I broke down and told them the truth.

"My mom is the one who shot him. She called me and told me what happened."

"Where is she now?"

"She's not here. She fled."

"Where did she go?" they pushed.

"I don't know."

They didn't seem convinced, but I was adamant. That visit from the police scared me so much. They weren't going to leave me alone. My entire neighborhood knew what had happened. Also, Eddie's family knew where I lived and it was only a matter of time before I heard from them. I started packing to move as soon as we got home and the police drove away. My mom was on the run and so were we.

I knew that my friend had a little, one-bedroom apartment for rent. I called and told her I had an emergency and needed to move in immediately. She agreed and we moved that same day. Anything that didn't fit in our cars was left behind. My sisters were home from Sonoma University on summer break, so there were five of us living in that tiny apartment.

That night everything changed for us. It was so traumatic. We were all just shell-shocked. The twins never returned to college. Our world was full of negative energy. We weren't innocent like other kids were. We'd seen too much in our lives. We were good kids, but we had been in this evil, conniving, lawless life for so long. We grew up without our fathers and now we would never have our mother. We were pretty much orphans now. It was devastating and life altering.

I couldn't relax, knowing that the police could show up at any time. They would show up at four o'clock in the morning. They'd come by and say that they were investigating something else and would ask if they could come in and look around. We always allowed them to search.

There was surveillance on my house, and they mistook my sister's mother-in-law for my mom. She looked quite similar to my mom, the same age, and the same body build and hair color. They followed her car and put their lights on her. They pulled her out of her car, and put her on the ground, spread-eagle with their guns on her before they realized their mistake.

My mother was featured on a show called "Placas," which was aired on the Spanish network. It was like America's Most Wanted. They showed our family picture and blurred out all our faces except my mom and baby brother, Adrian. The police had given them their version of events and said my mother could be armed and dangerous.

No one knew it at the time, but my mom was pregnant the night she killed Eddie and fled to Mexico; even she did not know. She had been in Tijuana for about four months when she began to feel the baby kick. I thought she should have an abortion because she and my brother were living in such a deplorable environment down there. She had a dilapidated, makeshift outdoor "room" with cement blocks stacked up and covered by a tarp. It was the size of a twin bed and all she had in it was a dirty mattress to sleep on. The bathroom was outside.

My nine-year old sister, Brenda, was living with me while my mom was in Tijuana. My mom called one day and said, "I need to see Brenda," so I drove her to visit on weekends. Brenda dreaded it, but my mom was insistent and I needed the reprieve from being in charge of a child. Every time I took her to my mother, Brenda would cry and beg me not to leave her there. It was heartbreaking.

After my mom had been a fugitive in Tijuana for several months, I got a call from her.

"I'm in San Diego. I just crossed the border."

By this time, she was nine months pregnant. She got a ride up to L.A. and went to stay with a friend. And then later she moved into the laundry room of an apartment building.

My brother Jesse was born shortly after. She was able to have him at Freeman Hospital, by giving them fake information about herself. Jesse's birth certificate doesn't have any real names on it. She gave a false name for herself, the father, and the baby.

When my mother and Jesse were released from the hospital, my sisters and brother and I went to see them in the room where she was living. When we visited her we would all sit on her mattress because the room was too small for anything else. She was restricted to the laundry room. From there she moved to another place, and then another. She moved around all the time, just trying to keep the police from finding her.

She became extremely paranoid. Whenever she thought someone recognized her she would move again. She would fill up a friend's car with her blankets, her clothes, as much stuff as she could fit. She couldn't rent a truck, so every time she moved, she couldn't take the belongings that did not fit in her friend's car. Toys that were given to the kids at Christmas would have to be left behind, TVs and furniture were all abandoned. Then she would start all over again. In the five years that she was a fugitive, she must have moved at least 40 times.

I constantly felt that I was being followed. I was very careful about what I said, even on the phone. The stress of that time was unreal. How do you live a normal life when you are forever looking over your shoulder, feeling like the roof could cave in at any second?

Naturally, the paranoia made my mother reclusive. She would never go out at night. The youngest kids, the boys, had never seen the darkness of night until they came to live with me. My mom had almost no resources to live on. She always lived in these little spaces with no bathrooms. She didn't want to impose on people, so she didn't shower regularly. She smelled of urine and her health was waning. It was an impossible situation.

Then there were my brothers. Adrian was six years old and had never been to school. She promised us that she would turn herself in as soon as Jesse could speak, but when that time came, she didn't want to leave them. One day, she told my sister Jeanette that she wanted to kill herself. She said that she thought she should kill herself and take the boys with her. Something had to be done.

Finally, in 2001, my mother was at a bus stop with the boys. A police officer approached her.

"Are you Rosa?"

"Yes," came her simple reply. She knew the chase was over. She was just done.

"How do you feel?"

"Relieved," she sighed.

She had been so desperate. After she had told Jeanette that she was thinking of killing herself and possibly the boys, it had been the last straw. Jeanette was in therapy and she told her therapist about it, and the therapist helped my sister to turn our mother into the police.

Chapter 8: Aftershocks

"Forgiveness is giving up the hope that the past could have been any different." - Oprah Winfrey

After my mom got busted, we needed to decide where the boys would live. We all wanted them. My older sister Claudia wanted them, I wanted them. The twins, Jeanette and Rosie wanted them too, but they were both single and didn't have their lives together. Jeanette was in rehab and therapy and Rosie was always moving around. Claudia was married and had 3 kids, and I was married and had only one daughter. In the end, because I was the closest to them, they came to live with me. I raised them myself, and all the while my mom was in jail. Growing up, I was always telling my mom that her kids were her responsibility, and yet in the end I chose to take them on myself. The irony is not lost on me. At that time I was 27 years old, going to school for my Associates Degree, and working for a big law firm as a legal secretary.

I hired a lawyer for my mom, but I didn't have much money, so I got what I paid for. The lawyer had been a teacher for 25 years and decided to become a lawyer, so he had only been working in law for three years. When we went to court he lost all his motions and arguments, and so we begged my mom to take a deal. My mom wanted to go to trial and tell her story so the jury would know what had happened. We pleaded with her not to do that, because if it went wrong, she would go to jail for the rest of her life.

After a lot of arguments, she finally agreed to a deal and was sentenced to 21 years. She got 11 years for the homicide, and 10 additional years for using a gun. It turned out that she was sentenced incorrectly, so I helped her appeal with my employer's help. This was during a time when there was a lot of scandal regarding dirty cops planting evidence, and sure enough, the police on my mother's case were some of them. We weren't able to prove that they had done anything wrong, but because she had been sentenced incorrectly, they lowered her time in jail by five years.

My husband, Frank, and I had been married for three years at this point and were raising our daughter, Frances. She was just two years old and brought a lot of joy and happiness to us. We were happy and excited with the life we were building. We had just bought our first home; a cute fixer upper in Whittier. Frank knew my mom's story and he was supportive, though he didn't tell his parents about it because he thought they would judge me. He actually didn't introduce me to his parents until one month before our wedding.

Frank was very put out when my brothers came to live with us. He took care of the kids while I was going to school. He was always unhappy, it was almost like he hated them. There was a financial strain; we were barely making it. We had money for food and rent, but with two more kids in the house, there was nothing extra. There would be no dinners out, trips to Magic Mountain, or weekends away. Every so often Frank would try to convince me to go out and leave the boys behind and I thought that was so mean. So then we wouldn't ever go out and we never had a break. We were always home with no reprieve.

Claudia helped occasionally, but she complained that she already had three kids and couldn't handle two more. Everyone had claimed to want these boys, but when it came down to it, I didn't get much help. I asked Claudia if she could alternate weekends with the boys so we could have a break, but it rarely happened. Our home was a very stressful place. My husband was constantly angry and pouty and I didn't like that side of him at all.

"You're so miserable." I said, "Two little boys ruin your whole life? How small are you?"

For two years it went on like that. If one of my brothers left their bike out or made too much noise, I would hear, "Punish them, Hazel! Hit them!"

"Frank, they are little boys. They are going to do what boys do. I'm not going to hit them."

"Why not call your mom, and find out if you were a quiet little kid? I just hate when the house is so noisy. I hate it when I come in and their shoes are thrown around in the living room."

These little things that all kids do were just unbearable to him. He had never been like this with our own daughter, who was only two-years old when the boys came to live with us. We had been happy. I had never seen him this intolerant or short-tempered before. We had stopped making love, in the bedroom and in every other sense. He wasn't mean to me, but he wasn't nice either. He was just flat and insensitive, day-in, day-out.

Once my brother ran in the house crying because Frank had yelled at him. Adrian had been watching Frank work on his car in the garage and when my husband noticed him there he bellowed at him to get out.

"I was just watching," sobbed Adrian. He was so upset, I couldn't stand it anymore. The peace I was trying so hard to keep in my house was tearing me apart. I comforted my brother and then stormed out to the garage.

"How could you be so mean, Frank? What if something happened to your parents and your sister and brother had to come and live with us?"

"I don't know what I would do if that happened," he said quietly, "but I can't help it. I'm not happy."

I know now that I was in the wrong in our relationship too. I didn't know how to be a wife and mother. It was Frank's mother who taught me about mothering. I didn't know how to care for a baby.

My mother-in-law did everything for my daughter. She bathed her, she fed her, when Frances got sick I left her with Frank's mother. I didn't know what I was doing, I wasn't ready, I was not inclined, and most of all, I hadn't learned from my own mother. I will always be grateful to Frank's mother who was a wonderful role model and taught me how to care for my baby.

As for Frank, I just didn't listen to him. I stopped paying attention to him when he behaved negatively. I took care of our daughter and my brothers and his needs were set firmly on the back burner. My brothers required a lot of attention, and I felt for them, not having their mother. I tried to make it up to them. Meanwhile, I was ignoring my husband. I didn't see it at the time, but it was true.

No one was happy. I wanted to leave my husband and I hated being home. At one point I even called the "Dr. Laura" radio show and they actually aired the call. I said, "I feel like I rescued my brothers to give them a better life, but what if I'm ruining their lives, because my husband is so mean?" Then she told me, in her snippy, sharp voice, "What's the alternative? Now you're going to have three kids without a father?" Is that what you want? Three kids without a father? Now your daughter will have no father? No, you have to suck it up. You have to suck it up and deal with it. Your daughter needs her father."

I thought, "Bullshit, Dr. Laura," and I left him.

I talked to him first. Frank was really a good guy, he had a lot of fine qualities, but he just couldn't handle the boys. He was only 25 years old and a bit immature. I didn't know how to handle the boys much more than he did, but if my life had taught me anything, it was that you do what you have to do to make things work. We parted without dramatics.

Part 2: The Miracles

Chapter 9: What's Your Sob Story?

"Some people create their own storms and then get upset when it rains." – Unknown

More than ten years after that violent, horrible night when my mother shot Eddie was when I attended that first personal development conference. After hearing all of the stories from the attendees, I was finally able to acknowledge my own sob story. I had a whole new perspective. It was as if I had been under water my entire life and suddenly I was on dry land with sure footing. Suddenly I knew that I would have a much richer life if I was able to be proactive. I could go out and get what I wanted, rather than just accepting things as they were. I had never looked at the future before and it rocked me.

I had gone to school and earned several degrees, but that was really because my boss pushed me. I never would have gone on my own. When I was interviewed for my job as a legal secretary, the attorney, Edward Ortega (no relation) asked me, "You're in college, right?" I said, "Yes," but I was not in college. I was married. I was raising three kids. I was in my mid-twenties, and I didn't even have a high school diploma. My dad always told me, "Fake it till you make it." I was hired, and I started working.

Shortly after, attorney Ortega asked me what classes I was taking, and so I told him I was on summer break at the moment. Then I knew I had to register for school. I thought if I just registered, I could tell him what classes I had, and he would leave me alone. Then he started asking me what I was learning in my classes. I was like, "Oh, my God. Now I have to pay attention in my classes?" Every semester, he did this. *Every* semester, he asked me, "What classes? What are you learning?"

Eventually, the day came when I got my Associate's degree. I was feeling great because finally this man would have to leave me alone. Later he came to me and asked, "What are you going to do next?"

I said, "I'm done. I just wanted to be a well-rounded person. I'm happy working for you, and I can see myself here forever."

He looked at me and said, "Oh, no. You're going to be a professional. Think about what you want to do."

I was like, "Oh, my God. This man is never going to leave me alone!"

He later told me, "My wife is a teacher, and she says there's a demand for bilingual school psychologists. That's what you should do. You should be a bilingual school psychologist."

I looked into the program, and I started taking psychology classes, which I liked a lot. Pretty soon, I earned my Bachelor's degree and eventually my Master's degree in educational psychology. At each of my graduations, my boss was there, my AA degree, my Bachelor's degree, and my Master's degree. He challenged me, and he cheered me on. He was right there every step of the way. I didn't invite this in, and if I'd been asked if I wanted to further my education on my own, I would have been completely uninterested.

Sometimes it takes a pushy person to be your angel and to make all the difference in your world. My life was transformed. If I had not gone to school, I would be working 40 plus hours a week and have little freedom. I would have a lot of bills and the stress of just barely making it. I would be living paycheck to paycheck and renting, like most everyone else I knew. Instead, today, I am an entrepreneur with many businesses. The best part is, not only did I graduate from college and become a professional, but my daughter is in college and thriving. Education was the key to escaping poverty and breaking the vicious cycle.

Even so, after I graduated, I wanted to keep my job as a legal secretary. I had all of this education and I still had no vision for the future. My boss-angel pushed me out of the nest this time. He said, "No. You're going to move on. You have to go. I hate to see you go, but you need to go."

It was terrifying! I was so blinded by where I came from, that I thought I had hit the ceiling of where my life could go. I thought that was as good as it would get for me. But when I started to see that I could shape my life by taking action, not just allowing things to happen to me, the blinders were lifted. I started thinking about how I had learned to accept limited and defeated behavior from my mother and I began to resent her. She could have left Eddie when he began to hit her, but her way was to deal with it. She put up with his abuse and endured it rather than cutting him out of her life. For example, if he was drunk and abusive when he came home at night, then she would just go to bed before he got there so he couldn't bother her. The example she set was one of an enabling, passive victim. I don't think it ever occurred to her that she could have just told him to take a hike.

I even confronted my mom about this, saying, "Why didn't you leave him? You didn't have to be in that situation! Why did you choose to stay?" I had begun to see that everything was a choice. I saw decisions where I had never noticed them before, but my mom was still in the dark. She couldn't see any way that life could have been different for her. I had moved a couple of steps forward, but she stood firmly in victim-mode.

My eyes were opening to the possibilities in my life. During this time, my dad called me to pick him up at the park. I hadn't seen him in a long time. He had not seen me pregnant and didn't meet my daughter until several months after she was born. When he got in the car, it was obvious that he was high. I introduced him to her, saying, "This is Frances, your granddaughter." He gazed at her vacantly and said, "He's so cute." He was out of it. He was so high that he couldn't see that she was a girl.

Then he said, "Take him to play in the park. I'll be right back."

I pushed Frances on the swings for a while, but my dad was taking a long time and I wasn't sure what to do. We walked back to the car and I sat there, wondering if I should leave him there. Just then he came running toward my car. I could see he was bleeding. He threw the door open and piled in yelling, "Go! Go! Go!"

"What happened?" I asked, completely shocked.

"Just go! Move!"

I pulled away from the park and he told me he'd been in a fight. It obviously had something to do with a drug deal. I was furious--and this was new to me. I had driven my dad to the park before on similar errands and I had never thought anything of it. Previously, I didn't realize I had the ability to choose *not* to take him. But now, I understood that he had chosen to put me, my baby daughter, and himself in danger. My mother had chosen to put us all in danger by choosing him to be my father. It was time that I chose to enforce some boundaries. This kind of crap did not have to take place in my life. I would not sit back and take it any longer.

I told my dad, "If you're only going to be calling me to ask for rides or money, don't. Don't call me. I'm not going to answer your calls." Maybe he understood, or maybe he just disappeared on his own. I don't know, but I held that boundary, and it gave me power.

I started to see choice everywhere. "My crazy life" was not a predetermined destiny. If I wanted a sob story, mine was as good as or better than anyone else's. I hadn't had it easy by any stretch of the imagination and I could cash in on that story until the wheels came off. It could be my excuse forever if that's all I wanted. But I wanted more, and everything was possible.

Small things occurred to me that I had never noticed before. I realized that I had never been to a bank with my mother as a child. I don't think she ever wrote a check in her life. In fact, when she did get a bit of money, she would make a little hole in the wall of our apartment and put the cash inside and then cover it over with spackling paste. When she needed the money she'd break it open and cover the hole up again. Our whole apartment was full of these little holes. I have no idea how she could remember where the money was.

I used to "float" checks as a means of getting by. When payday was on Friday, I could start writing checks on Wednesday and they would take a few days to post so I would cross my fingers and hope that the timing worked out. Of course, that was a horrible plan and I often bounced checks because my boss would pay me late or the bank would put a hold on the money. I was living "below" paycheck to paycheck like so many others do. It was the way I survived; barely keeping my head above water.

When I was 19 I got my first checking account because my boss paid me with checks. I had previously been taking them to a check cashing service, but my boss suggested I open an account so I wouldn't have to pay the outlandish fees that check cashing places charge. With a checking account I bounced checks, and I had to pay fees for them, but at least I had the ability to get groceries when I didn't have any money. I knew how long different places would take to cash a check. Low on gas and broke? The drugstore takes a week to cash a check so you're safe. My car would get impounded for having too many parking tickets so I would just write a check to cover it. Sometimes the bank would close my account because I was overdrawn, and I would go open another one. I probably did that five times.

I had never experienced the act of saving money, it was just about getting enough money to survive. I never thought about having a cushion or safety net. I focused on the amount I needed to make to pay for rent, my gas, my utilities, and maybe a little extra money for fun. I didn't look any further into the future than that; I was conditioned into a poverty mentality.

As I began to look at myself and improve my life, I took a money seminar. There I realized how much money I was throwing away by bouncing checks. I guess I had buried my head in the sand. Bouncing 15 checks and paying a fee of $20 for each is $300! I just flushed that money.

Besides the amount of wasted money, I had to check my integrity. I had previously thought of banks as inhuman, so who cares? They can wait for their money. Getting straight with my finances meant getting straight with my honor and morals, so the bounced checks stopped. Now, if I write you a check, that's me honoring my word.

Once you recognize your sob story and move away from being its victim, there will be anger. Even as you have amazing realizations that there is a world of choice and opportunity right in front of you, it will piss you off too, because that world has been there all along and you couldn't see it! It is important that you let that anger happen so you can move beyond it. I demanded answers from my mom and I blamed her for not giving me a better example to follow, but then I realized blame was useless and wholly unsatisfying. It just was what it was. I was grown and the people who were supposed to raise me were no longer responsible for forming me. That was on me now. I picked up the phone and made amends with my sisters. I contacted my ex-husband and owned up to my part of the problems in our marriage. I took responsibility for the choices I had made and for what I had brought to the relationships in my life.

Before I ditched my sob story I thought college was for *other people*, not for me. Then my angel of a boss gave me the encouragement and resolve to get a strong education which has opened countless doors for me.

I once thought I could only have a life of marriage and motherhood. Then I left a safe, but troubled marriage to strike out on my own and in doing so, became an example for my children.

I thought earning enough money to cover my bills was good enough and the only reason to work. Then I followed my dreams, founded businesses and organizations and I take pride in my ideas, accomplishments, and in the plentiful living I have created for myself and my family.

The transition goes like this:

1. You realize that you have been the victim of your life story.
2. You get angry when you see that this story has held you back.
3. You begin to see choices in all parts of life that you had never noticed before.
4. You make amends with the people you have blamed for your place in life.

Once this transition takes place, real miracles can happen.

My values really came into focus as I went through this change. Honesty and integrity were of utmost importance. I was dating a man who was separated but not divorced from his wife. I knew that could not continue. I was not honoring my beliefs both by passively accepting his situation and by being a part of what I considered a dishonest relationship. When I realized this I told him, "This is not right. Either you get a divorce or we end this."

Do you know what he said to me?

"I'm impressed with your new found integrity."

Unbelievable.

So we broke up.

I began to see where I had made choices to accept or take part in activities that were straight up wrong. I had lied and cheated and certainly been part of some questionable activities. I had never once thought about this before. It was just the way things happened. I see now that when I did these things I was in survival mode, so of course I wasn't being honest. I had a sob story and that blinded me to my wrong doing. I was able to use my story as fuel and reason to do anything I "had" to do. When you are attached to your sob story you can't live in integrity because the story has brainwashed you into thinking that things have to be a certain way and you are forced to operate within those circumstances any way you can. I didn't have any guilt or remorse for lying or cheating because I never even gave it any thought. Consequences, other people's feelings--I didn't consider them at all. I was numb inside.

There is an expression in Texas: "You gotta rise above your raisin'." This means you have to believe that you are capable of changing to live a better life than the one you grew up in. You can behave in a way that is incongruous with your family or upbringing. This is possible for all of us, no matter how dismal your situation may have been.

As your values come into focus, you will learn how to function within them, rather than the way you have been functioning around your sob story. As I was segueing into living by my values, I asked myself what I wanted, and I remember very clearly feeling grateful to my mother for being home with me when I was a young child. I had never appreciated that before, but it was the first and strongest thing that came to my mind. I wanted that for my own daughter. I wanted her to be able to count on me being there if she was sick. She wouldn't have to go to school sick or stay with a babysitter; she would be with me. This gave me even more inspiration and power to design my life.

I began to see that I had been conditioned to have low expectations of myself and of the world around me. I felt unworthy of anything better than where I came from. My mom had no education, seven children from different men, and my father, a gangster, dropped out of school in 9th grade. That made it scary for me to be around educated people. I was terrified to be in a situation where I had to be around educated people. I would freeze, afraid that they would ask me a questions I couldn't answer. Our parents are our first teachers in that they are the people who instruct us about how the world works and how we should react to it. I realized that my parents, with their very limited view of the world, were the people I had gone to for guidance my entire life. That was a big wake up for me! I felt like the ground was slipping from beneath my feet and that everything I thought about the world was not real, not true.

One story I told myself was that I was not loving, because my mom didn't hug me and didn't show affection. Then I figured out that wasn't true at all, it was just a story I had been telling myself. If I am not receiving love it is because I am not giving love. I need to reach my hand out and be loving and affectionate. I thought I would always be deprived of love, but then I saw where I had been withholding love. I stubbornly suppressed love toward my sisters, my daughter, my husband, my mom, and others.

Whatever you are missing in your life is what you are not putting in. Your story isn't over. You get to write the new chapters. You choose the characters, you choose the theme. Yours is a story only you can tell.

VIP RESOURCE:

Visit www.themasteryofmiracles.com/vip-resources to download a free worksheet and guided audio to take you through the Mastery of Miracles visioning process.

Chapter 10: Letting People In

"Vulnerability is the birthplace of innovation, creativity and change." — Brené Brown

Once I saw the responsibility I had for the quality of my relationships, it was time to make amends. The story I had previously been telling myself about my sister, Claudia was that she was a lousy sister. She was the oldest and should bear the most responsibility to help in the family. She was letting me down, which gave me the right to call her a bitch, to bad mouth her to other people, to withhold love from her, and to judge her. I believed that my older sister was always supposed to take care of me and help me with my problems. When she said "no," it pissed me off. I couldn't see that she was setting her own boundaries to keep herself out of the craziness we grew up in. She had three children to care for and I was the one who had taken on my brothers, not her. She was the first kid to leave our mother's house and she made a new life for herself. I was still caught up in my mom's drama and problems and I thought I didn't have a choice about that. In my mind I was supposed to give in to whatever was needed, I thought I was required to help my mother no matter what. Claudia would not get involved in my mother's antics--her drugs, her men, her choices. My sister had closed that chapter for herself. I see now that I probably secretly envied her ability to separate herself, but at the time I was outraged. I labeled her a terrible sister and daughter. I tortured us both over that.

When I was at the personal development conference and they wanted me to call Claudia and tell her about my new insights, I was so scared. My family didn't talk about feelings. No one ever apologized or took responsibility for anything. That was for other people--TV families like the Brady Bunch. We didn't communicate that way. If my sister and I had a fight, three days later we would see each other and we would never bring it up. On the surface we were just moving on, but underneath the resentment was still all there, eating away at us.

I was at the front of the room at the conference and the speaker told me to call Claudia. I began to make excuses right away.

"I can't call her. She's in Mexico."

"They don't have phones in Mexico?" the speaker chided. "Go call your sister and come back and let me know how it went."

There was no way out, so I dialed her number and held my breath. When she answered the phone, I stumbled through the call in tears.

"Hi. I'm at this personal development seminar, and I'm working on myself."

"What's going on, Hazel?" she asked, obviously confused.

"Well, I realize that I've been treating you like you were a bitch all this time because when we were growing up, mom told me that you were supposed to take care of me. When we were kids, you did take care of me. But when we grew up, I still thought it was your job to take care of me. So even when you did something nice for me, I just expected it as owed to me. You gave me a car, you paid part of my rent, and you threw me the best bridal shower I have ever been to. I don't think I even said 'thank you.' My wedding was at your home and I robbed you of the gratitude I should have shown. You did so much and I was so ungrateful. All I could see were the times you said 'no' to me. I just want you to know that I am so sorry. I am going to be a better sister. You don't have to do anything for me. You're a perfect sister and I love you."

Everything came gushing out like a dam had broken. I let her know that I realized how bratty and unfair I had been with her when she wouldn't help me with our brothers. I told her how I had complained about her and resented her every time she told me "no." I let her know that it was my issue for believing that as my older sister, she was responsible for me.

Claudia took a moment and said, "Hazel, stop crying. Just stop! You don't have to tell me these things." It was as if she couldn't take it; she was overwhelmed. We had never spoken like this. In my family, taking responsibility was completely foreign. Acknowledgement? Never!

From that point forward, everything changed for us. I stopped anticipating her refusal of any favor I asked. I had no idea that I was manifesting all the times she turned me down by expecting it! I detached from the expectation and that gave her the freedom to help me when she was able, but to know that it was not a big deal if she couldn't help.

It's so difficult to shift from placing blame anywhere but on yourself to admitting where you are responsible. That call to my sister was a door that had to be opened in order for me to become an authentic person. I had to forgive us both and look at the reality, not the story I had created to feel righteous. It was horrendous, but it was perfect and I wanted more.

The change in my perspective made me more aware overall. It was almost like I was watching a movie of the story of my life, but there was this thing I had been missing the first time through, and now I saw it. Instead of only seeing it from my own point of view, I was able to see it from many different points of view; the views of the other people in my life. This was an incredible awakening for me; I had only ever seen things my way before.

One of the (many) other calls I made was to my cousin, Dora. There had been bad blood between us for a long time at that point. Many years prior, she had borrowed three thousand dollars from me. I had not yet learned that I shouldn't loan money I couldn't afford to lose. I wasn't earning a lot at that time and raising my daughter and brothers was expensive but she promised to pay me back within a couple of weeks. She put me off when I asked to be repaid, and not only was it very inconvenient, it felt disrespectful. Resentment grew in me every time she told me it would just be two more weeks before she could pay me back.

After a year of being blown off, I decided to take her to court. I was working in the law office, so I knew how it was done. Who knows if I ever would have thought of doing this if I had worked in another kind of business? I filed a suit and I didn't feel obligated to keep the details to myself when it came to my family. Everyone knew how I felt she had screwed me over.

That's where it got even uglier. I had brought shame upon my family by bringing in a lawyer. It was not acceptable to bring an outsider to family matters. That is not done. My Uncle Ruben, Dora's father, was furious with me, saying I had betrayed my cousin. He was embarrassed that she had not paid me and now the whole family knew about it because I had laid it all out in the open. There was so much drama and bad energy that even if she had the money, I can see why she wouldn't want to pay me.

Dora and I had been like sisters growing up, so when I began calling people to make amends, she was high on the list. Several years had passed. Enough was enough. I could have been more patient with her. We didn't have to end up in court. She didn't pick up my call, so I left a message explaining my fault in what had happened. I'm sure my message was way too long, but it all needed to be said. I finally saw the bigger picture and the impact my actions had on our relationship and all of our mutual relationships.

"Dora," I began, "I want to apologize for what happened. I could have been more understanding. I could have come to you for a conversation rather than allowing myself to get so angry that I took you to court. I could have been discreet and kept the issue between the two of us. I know I made the problem worse. I remember when we used to play Barbie's together as kids. I love you and I miss having you in my life. My daughter is growing up and I want you to know her. I want to know you and your kids. I want us to be a family again. You are the link to that happening. I miss your mom too, she was like a second mother to me. There is an entire side of the family that we are missing out on. I am not the same person I was. I am not a threat to you, and if you'll give me the chance, I'll show you that."

Dora was not having it. She didn't call me back, instead she texted me. "Hey Hazel, I heard your message. I don't hate you anymore but i don't want anything to do with you."

That is going to happen sometimes. Just because someone doesn't accept your apology, it doesn't make the act of owning up to your mistakes any less valuable. By being courageous enough to face your part in the things that haven't worked in your life, you are honoring your values. This sort of thing can take time and ultimately, some people are simply unwilling to forgive, which is their right. Don't dwell on it. Work to avoid making the same mistakes in the future and to create strong relationships.

I replied back, "I respect that, and I appreciate your response. I'm here and ready when and if you want to come back together." After that, I would send her a Facebook message whenever I thought of her. "Today is your birthday and I am thinking about you," and things like that. For five years I got no response, but I kept doing it.

When my mother died, we were all shocked to see Dora at the funeral service. We had a reception at my house afterward and she and her kids came to that as well. The last time I had seen those kids they were three and one-year old and here they were, 18- and 15-years old. It had been 15 years, but suddenly we became a family again.

Dora texted me a few days later and told me that she had been in therapy. "For a long time I have felt that something is missing in my life, but I didn't know until just now that what was missing was you."

I feel very fortunate that she and I were able to come back together. However, even if we had not, taking responsibility restored my integrity. I didn't hold anything back. When you approach someone with a confession of culpability, they are not obligated to accept it, regardless of your fine intentions. You will not always get a happy ending. Respect their position and they may come to you later, or not. Either way, you have honored your values and life will go on.

As you become more comfortable having these difficult conversations, it will become part of the way you handle your life on a more ongoing basis. These admissions and communications will happen in the small moments instead of after a problem has grown and festered.

I have these moments frequently in my personal and professional life. If I sense a misunderstanding or conflict developing, I stop, share my thoughts and give the other person an opportunity to correct me or give their own opinion. Clearing the air consistently creates peace and harmony in all areas of life. When you let people in, you allow yourself to see and release any shame, guilt, and judgement that you hold. You create a safe space for others to do the same which brings more community to your life. You model the behavior you want to encourage and share it with the people in your life so they can be inspired to introduce this kind of communication and authenticity to their other relationships.

While I fully believe that letting people in improves my quality of life exponentially, I will give you a note of caution. Be safe with yourself. If you feel in your body that having a difficult conversation will escalate or become volatile, set some ground rules. Be mindful of who you are sharing with, ask for their confidentiality and consider involving a mediator or therapist if you feel that the conversation will go awry. Everyone needs to feel safe.

Chapter 11: Are You Living Groundhog Day?

"Don't think. Act. We can always revise and revisit once we've acted. But we can accomplish nothing until we act." — Steven Pressfield

As you move through this book and perhaps identify your own sob stories, begin to let people in, and endeavor some difficult conversations, things can get stormy. You may feel as if you are taking two steps forward and three steps back. It can be frustrating. You may start to recognize when and where you fall into "autopilot" mode and revert back to old habits. You may be caught so tightly in behaviors and responses that you feel like you are living Groundhog Day; all those stories hold you in a loop.

In my situation, I never expected any day to look different from the day before. I couldn't see the future. Maybe I didn't even *believe* in the future. I didn't create anything--life just happened to me. I found myself in the same kind of bad relationships over and over again. I found one job I could do and planned to plant myself there for as long as they would have me.

Once you've busted one story you've been telling yourself that has been holding you back, you will begin to see more. You will begin to see the stories of other people. One sure way to determine whether a story is holding you back is when you think or say, any of the following:

That's just the way I am.
I have bad luck.
That's just the way things are.
This is what always happens to me.

There are many alternate thoughts that are just as limiting. When these thoughts pop up you have to call bullshit on them. Any of this kind of defeatist self-talk is what is keeping you in that loop and keeping you from seeing the miracles and unlocking change in your life. It takes action to get out and get what you want. If you can't see forward, you'll keep doing the things you have always done and get the same results. You can only create the life you want by looking forward.

Small changes are the way to start. Push yourself by making different choices like taking a different route to work, trying a new recipe, or ordering something different than usual at lunchtime. All of the ruts you stay in affect how you feel, how much energy you have, and how you show up in all the areas of your life. Begin a new story!

Say something new. Start conversations with people that are different than the usual chit chat. For example, I speak with my sisters a lot, and I can predict how the conversations will go. We talk about day-to-day stuff. I never initiate a conversation with them about art or endurance swimming or anything creative. I'm sure if I say something different, we will have different conversations. I mentioned this to my sister, Brenda the other day and she told me she is a writer and loves to write poems. I had no idea! She shared her writing with me and she is very talented. If I had never brought this up I would still not know about the gift she has. This kind of change could spark something remarkable and open new doors in your relationships.

The loops you can get caught up in can be in relationships, career, anything really. As I've mentioned earlier, growing up we were not taught how to cook. We ate a lot of junk. Ramen noodles, fast-food, and cereal. My mom didn't allow us to cook because she thought we would burn ourselves, as she had done when she was a child (there's one of *her* loops!). When I moved out on my own, I kept this up. I bought microwavable food or food that could be boiled easily. Then a boyfriend taught me how to make spaghetti, so that was added once or twice a week. After decades of eating this way, my body started to rebel. I got sick easily, I caught a lot of colds. I was anemic and had very low energy. I gained weight and I felt like an old lady inside a young woman's body.

Then one day I took my brother to see a doctor to be assessed for Attention Deficit Disorder (ADD), and get medication. The doctor told me she thought I may have ADD as well. She told me that my brother would function better if his diet was improved and that I would benefit from that too. She set me up with a health coach, Gemi who recommended cutting out processed foods and adding in foods like kale and beets. I thought it sounded disgusting! I had never tasted a beet or kale in my life. Vegetables were not part of my world; they were completely alien to me.

At 45 years old I finally saw that there was another way to eat and prepare food that would improve my life. I had always told myself that I didn't know how to cook and that the food I made never tasted good. I was still holding on to that story. When I started working with Gemi I was amazed at how good some of these new foods could be. She showed me how to make a delicious beet shake with blueberries, coconut oil, a bit of ginger and water. Kale can really taste bad, but if you massage lemon into it, it becomes less chewy and you can mix it into a salad. I began preparing meals for my family and my friends and they liked them. This has been a big step in my life and I see the results from the nutrition I have brought into my daily life.

In order to challenge my story of being an awful cook with no time to prepare food, I had to be open to seeing a different way of doing things when it was offered to me. When I was talking with the coach, I heard myself lying. Did I really believe that I *couldn't* learn to cook? Me, the woman who had gotten her master's degree, couldn't figure out how to use an oven? Really? I was full of it and I knew it. When I realized that, I asked her to help me.

The change was another big one. Gemi came into my home and helped me set up the kitchen with the tools and ingredients I needed. She taught me one recipe at a time. We took action together, but they were baby steps. As we moved along, more and more recipes and options were introduced. I stopped worrying about whether I could cook or not and just jumped in. Sometimes a small taste of success is all it takes to bust the myths you have created about yourself. We are all stronger and more capable than we think we are. Breaking out of the Groundhog Day loop will bring you more possibilities than you can currently imagine. No matter how much you evolve, there will always be room for more growth.

Chapter 12: The Lies You Tell Yourself

"Worse than telling a lie is spending your whole life staying true to a lie." - Robert Brault

Your words create your world. Words are incredibly powerful. It is important to be conscious about the words you use. It is like the law of attraction. What you put out is what you get back. If you talk about negative qualities, you will get more negativity in your life. When I used to speak of my sisters, I used words like "moody," "difficult," and "judgmental." I never talked about their kindness or how loving they are. I painted them with a negative brush and this came back to me in the form of distance and more difficulty with them. My words = my results.

I knew I wanted something different when it came to family relationships. I was in school and in my psychology master's program, I had to do ten hours of introspection each month. I did a lot of journaling and was prompted with questions like, "Where did you have a breakdown in your communication and what did you learn from it?" I learned about communication words in psychology and how to get people to open up and use their words to describe things. I noticed a lot of my own words like "That's hard," or "That's never going to happen."

Do you find yourself talking about how "Christmas time is hectic," or "Taxes are a nightmare,"? That's the kind of thing that will ensure a frenzied holiday or miserable tax season. These are not solid truths. Holidays and taxes are not inherently rough things. You have made a hard, predetermined judgement and brought it upon yourself.

We also tell ourselves lies about who we are and who the people in our lives think we are. I convinced myself that I was a very serious person who was not a lot of fun and had few friends. I thought that my family didn't understand me. I didn't think they could comprehend what it's like to run a company with employees, and have a vision for the future. I stepped away from my family and started to seclude myself. The more I thought about this, the more real it became. I proved myself right by believing the lies I was telling.

Then I realized I was buying into a bunch of crap! I wanted to see myself differently, so I set an intention and changed my behavior. I surprised my family by showing up to a birthday celebration to which I was not invited but I heard about on Facebook. My intention was to let the evening be easy and fun. I was not going to lug all of my lies around with me that night. It was a really enjoyable party and the next day my cousin texted me saying, "Oh my god, Hazel. You were so much fun last night." I wasn't over the top, I wasn't trying to be the life of the party I just showed up without all of my judgements.

I also became more vocal with love and praise. In my communication studies at school we were learning the importance of language and feelings. As a mother, I assumed that my daughter knew how much I loved her. I thought my actions were all she needed as proof of my love. In my mind I reasoned, "I'm your mother. I'm here. I pay the bills. You have a house. I take care of you. I changed your diapers, so you know I love you." But when I told her, "You're so smart and so beautiful. I can't believe you're my daughter," she stood up straighter and I could see she was happier. I started to say what I felt and I saw big change in my life. Even when my daughter would behave sassy or bratty, I learned to embrace it. I love her so much, I love seeing her be herself. I want to feed her greatness.

My family has a Facebook family chat group, so I used that to reach everyone. One day I wrote, "I have felt that you don't care about me; that you don't understand me, and that you distance yourself from me. I have felt that we have nothing in common and it seems like I'm alone. I have posted pictures and comments in our group and when nobody responded, I thought that nobody cared. And in reality, you do care and you love me so much. And I love you. And you guys have always been there for me and you're very supportive." Those words unlocked a flood of replies saying "We love you!"

When I leaned in to the positive thoughts, I pushed myself to stretch a bit more. I think it's a common default to think negatively and it takes work to shift that. The hardest part for me was changing my thinking habits. Acknowledging the people in my life in big and small ways has changed everything for me. What I think and say *does* make a difference.

Imagine you have a file cabinet that contains all of your words, everything you know, your experiences, your skills, your education, your physical abilities, and your capacity for love. Everything about you fits in one drawer, but there are 10 drawers you could fill. We have so much more ability, but most of us function at only 10 percent. Allow yourself to be above average.

Let's say a friend or colleague tells me, "Hazel, I really like your dress," and I reply, "Thank you so much for the compliment. It means a lot to me, especially coming from somebody whose style I admire." When I return the compliment and express the importance of their opinion, we all feel good. Genuine expression like this costs you nothing and is the kind of thing that will help you expand and fill up some of those other file cabinet drawers. In acknowledging the compliment and the person who gave it, there is an honesty that magnifies the love in your life.

I will caution you about the company you keep. When you find people who are cheerleaders for complaints or negativity, it may feel good to vent in the moment, but in the long run it feeds fear. If you spend time with people going over grievances and using words to validate and confirm them, they will expand and become more solid.

When I was growing up, all of my friends also believed that money was scarce. We talked about money problems a lot. We made it bigger and bigger. I remember hearing my own kids talk about how we didn't have money, because they heard me say it all the time. When I couldn't afford something they wanted instead of saying, "Not right now," or "You have plenty of toys," I would tell them there was no money.

One big social difference I see between people with money and people without much money is a deeply-rooted belief of wealthier people, that you are safe and no matter what happens things will be fine. Even if they are hit with a large, unexpected expense, they don't despair, because they know money will come back around. They can get fired, or have their belongings stolen, but it's OK. They don't go to that place of crazy pessimism and desperation because of a setback. This attitude is actually what keeps them calm and confident. It is as if they're psychologically conditioned to be optimistic, and of course it becomes a self-fulfilling prophecy.

Once things were looking up for me and my family I was flying high. My business was growing and I was making more money. The kids were doing well. I was traveling and I had just bought a new car. The kids were all driving and had cars. Life was going amazingly well.

I came home after work one day and walked out to grab the mail. Sitting in my mailbox were two letters. One from my mother and one from my father; both written from jail.

It was such a contrast to the life I had built for myself and a very big reality check for me. Here I was living an incredible life and no one outside of my family knew that my parents were both in jail. Would my colleagues and friends even believe me if I told them? From the outside I looked like I had lived a charmed life.

It was bittersweet, I suppose. I hated thinking of them in jail, but here I was, their daughter, creating a life I loved. I got out. I might have ended up where they did, but I chose another path. I was making a life that was not only fulfilling basic needs, but was well on its way to surpassing them.

You are creating your reality. If you want more money, be on the lookout for how many times you talk about not having any. If you don't want more money, keep complaining. Pay close attention to the words you use. This is not easy, but be diligent and catch yourself when you are withholding kindness or assuming negative ideas. When you change your operating system, you get to live a bigger, better life. It's like turning your life from black and white into brilliant Technicolor.

Chapter 13: Fear is a Roadblock for Everything You Want

"Miracles start to happen when you give as much energy to your dreams as you do to your fears." - Richard Wilkins

With all of the ideas I have been sharing with you in the previous chapters, this point is where fear likes to creep in and get really loud. The lies you have been telling yourself are being called out and released. Those lies were a form of self-protection and without them you may be feeling vulnerable. You may even feel paralyzed. That's completely normal and this is the time to find healthy ways to deal with fear instead of coming up with more lies or rolling back to your sob stories that do not serve you. Getting to the other side of fear is not easy, but I promise that it is worth the tough things you need to do to get there.

Because I grew up poor, I had a strong fear of not having money. I had never learned how to save money and I lived in a state of scarcity and lack, scrambling and not looking ahead. When I got out on my own, I never actually lost my home, but I came close, owing months of back mortgage payments. I was terrified of having no home. It was constant.

Growing up, when the bills weren't paid, we had to shower at the recreational center, at my aunt's place, or sometimes, just go without any shower at all. We washed clothes and tennis shoes in the kitchen sink or bathtub and dried our shoes in the oven. There was a lot of shame in not having the basic necessities. As I grow older, the fear persists. Even though I have made money, this fear clings on. When I notice it popping up, I pull myself away from it by creating opportunities or a vision for the future. I realize I need to do something to make myself feel good about the future.

I have enough money now, *if* nothing changes, but my fear is that something crucial will change and I'll be depleted again. The fear is still with me, but now I have some tools to help me climb out of it. I immediately change my thought. Let's say you get a large and unexpected bill and it is upsetting and overwhelming. This is not the time to deal with that bill. You are not in a healthy place to take action when you are in fear. For now, change your activity. Take a walk, check your email, play with your dog, go to the gym, or pick up the phone and call a friend. This does not mean ignoring the bill, but give it a little space and don't try to tackle it when you are upset. When you come back to this bill, you will approach it in a different way, from a better place.

Fears will crop up throughout life. Certain people or places can trigger fear. It is helpful just to acknowledge when you are feeling fear and what is causing it. When you understand where it is coming from, it is easier to stay calm. Keep a constant awareness and know that as George Addair said, "everything you have ever wanted is on the other side of fear." Remind yourself of what is good in your life. Affirm the other side of the coin; the things that are working. There is always something working. You are alive. You are breathing right now. Change the channel and explore gratitude.

Think about what you want. What scares you about it? As you answer these questions, it is like poking fear out of the corner. Shine some light on the fear. Find out what makes it tick. Invite fear out to play. When you delve into understanding it, you will lessen its power.

As I cautioned in the last chapter, the company you keep is very important. We can create a climate of fear if we are not mindful. Entire communities, friendships, and social circles can be built on fear which is dangerous because fear becomes more solid when it is validated in groups. It can be difficult to see anything else.

It may be helpful to take an inventory of all of your relationships and the places you spend time. Notice if they are expanding your fears. If they are, it could be time to make some changes. People suffering from disappointment and regret may be raging against what they consider "fate." Growing up around my peers and adults who constantly complained about being broke, gossiped about others, and cried the blues about the injustice of things, made me believe that my future was very limited.

I signed up for a seminar about handling money because I knew I needed to work on my beliefs about it. I had been making the same amount of money in my business for five years and I was barely getting by. I was still bouncing checks, even in my business. I bounced checks to colleagues and people I respected.

What I learned in that seminar is that I was creating my own future and my dreams were all within my means. I didn't dream of yachts and mansions or luxury trips around the world, I dreamt of buying a modest SUV and being debt-free. I didn't aim to be wealthy. I was not thinking of abundance. I put a lid on myself. I didn't believe I was worthy of big dreams. I didn't think I was smart enough to make that much money.

When I realized that I was stunting my own growth, I saw where I was not taking the actions necessary to grow my business to its potential. I wasn't doing what needed to be done. I was afraid to hire a coach or attend seminars because I thought there was not enough money for it. However, when I invested in coaching and seminars and learned how to create space to make more money. I learned to invite it in.

Part of this learning was the content of the work, but another part was the community I put myself in. The people around me were creating possibility, not lamenting what they did not have. We constantly asked ourselves, "What if I was brave and did it anyway?" Instead of being surrounded by a world full of "Isn't it awful?" and "We'll never move beyond this place in life," I had a fellowship of people helping me expand rather than contract and shut down. It felt wonderful.

Dealing with certain people from my life before I found this community became difficult. I had moments when I stepped away from negative friends. I literally walked away from conversations and stopped spending time with some of them. I had the contrast of feeling uplifted in this new community and I just couldn't put myself in negative situations if I wanted to keep growing.

I spent a lot of time alone. I didn't make time for my original friends. My phone didn't ring. I had nothing to do and a lot of time and it was lonely. I like to golf, I like to travel, and I had no one to do those things with me. My coach told me to step into the community of people who were helping me expand. I was scared because it felt like a big step and I wasn't sure they would accept me, but I got brave and did it anyway.

Some of my old friends have drifted back into my life in a different way than they were before. When you are making changes, it is easy to make judgements about the people you are no longer jibing with. There's a certain level of less-than and more-than thinking. Now I realize that we are all equally divine beings and I have more tolerance and understanding. It's as if I have built up a bank account of positivity and now that I am stronger, I can allow myself back into some of my former communities because I can take control now and not be pulled under.

I had dinner with an old friend who I don't see much anymore. She's almost 50 years old and she was complaining about her job. She's also in college to become a nurse.

"Come on," I said. "You're almost 50 and you haven't even become a Certified Nurse Assistant. What are you doing in school?"

She looked at me and blurted, "This is why I don't hang out with you, because you make me feel bad about myself."

"How am I making you feel bad about yourself? Every time I see you, you complain about work and I've told you about the CNA program which is only six to nine months long and you could get your license and be making more money than you are now at a job you hate."

"Yeah, but I have responsibilities," she said defensively.

"OK, I don't have to give you any more ideas. I can just go along with your complaining, but I have information that could help you and I don't want to withhold it from you. I am not trying to make you feel bad."

I knew I was done. Some people feel very safe in their fear. They hold onto injustices and judgements like a security blanket. They can use it as a reason for all of their shortcomings. They don't want to change.

So you may have to pull away from some of the people in your life in the beginning. When you stop complaining and start truth-telling, some people won't like it. When I started taking responsibility and being proactive in my life, my friends who liked to complain stepped away from me. When I challenged their complaints with solutions (Have no money? What are you going to do about it? Maybe you can take a part-time job on the side or go back to school and get new skills.) they avoided me. They just wanted to stay in their complaints. You can't expect anything to change that way. Waiting for a solution to fall into your lap is delusional. You can bring more of what you want to your life when you make a shift in who you spend your time with.

I went to another dinner with five women who were all complaining about how hard it is to find a man. I know that is all lies that they are creating and I was bored to death of the conversation; it was dominating the whole evening. I thought to myself, "I am here to experience the best life I can. I am not going to be bored at this table." I changed the subject by asking them, "So what have you been doing for fun lately?" They were full-blast into their pity party and I changed it just like that. The talk turned to something much more pleasant. When dinner was over I walked away thinking about how powerful it was to make that turn around. I don't have to sit there and be miserable. I hope that the women got something out of it too.

Separating yourself from people who drag you down doesn't have to be forever. People change. Who knows? You may come back to find that you have the power to pull some of them up with you. Some of them may have moved ahead on their own.

Cutting yourself away from fear is all about freedom. You can be free to see solutions you may never have considered before. It is part of growth and it can point you down undiscovered paths that lead you to adventure and joy.

VIP RESOURCE:

Visit www.themasteryofmiracles.com/vip-resources to download a free worksheet and guided audio to take you through the Mastery of Miracles visioning process.

Chapter 14: What are Your Intimate Relationships, or Lack of, Telling You About Yourself?

"Some people make you feel the opposite of lonely; they make you feel not only that you aren't as awful as you secretly fear you are, but in fact that you are more wonderful, more astonishing, more full of riches and wisdom and beauty than you ever would have thought possible." - Sally Franson

My family did not say "I love you" to one another. We learned that love was implied and didn't need to be vocalized. That had a long-lasting effect on me because I wasn't able to give verbal affirmations and share love freely to the people in my life. I was stingy with it. I could write "I love you," in letters and I could reply with it if someone said it to me first, but I could not initiate. I was protecting myself by being cold and distant.

My ex-husband was the first person who told me "I love you." At that time we had been dating about 3 months and he sent flowers with a card that said "I love you." I was stunned. *What? He loves me???* It was incredible to me because I was not there yet. I wasn't even thinking about loving someone. It meant a lot to me and I know I softened with him after that, but I did not return the "I love you." I don't think we ever said it out loud to one another during our marriage without it feeling weird to me.

The man I dated after my divorce was so open and free with loving words, that it honestly made me uncomfortable. I wanted to be loving with him, but I told myself the stupid lie that it "wasn't my way."

Once my brother was messing around with my phone and replied to a text from my boyfriend as if he was me. He wrote something like, "Baby, I can't wait to see you." I did not use that kind of language and "baby" is a word I would have never used with a man. When my boyfriend picked me up for dinner that night he said, "I just want to tell you that text really made my day."

"I have to confess, I'm not the one who sent that to you. My brother sent it," I said.

He got so angry with me, and he told me that he had been waiting for me to say words like that.

"Damnit, Hazel, why couldn't you just let me have that moment?"

But I wasn't ready to let him in.

I wasn't ready to let anyone in. I was cold and distant and I started to see that in all of my relationships. I was expecting love to show up to an inhospitable host. That was not going to happen. Then I took a class in the "Ask and Receive Method." I learned about *Asking God for What You Want.* I knew I had to rise for anyone to show up the way I wanted. The only thing preventing me from the relationships I desired was *me.*

I had a lot to learn. Once I understood that affection and openly caring were not weaknesses, I had to figure out how to show love. I knew if I wanted love in my life, I was going to have to embrace my ability to be loving.

In addition to romantic love, I had to learn to show love to my family, which was awkward for everyone in the beginning. When I made that first phone call to my sister Claudia from the personal development conference, my sobs, apologies, and declarations of love made her pretty uncomfortable. She kept telling me to stop and that she didn't need me to tell her I love her. We've all softened since then. I told myself that I wanted a happy, healthy relationship with my sister. I wanted us to thrive and have fun together. So I became more attentive to her. I was available to her. I gave her genuine compliments.

I got a text from Claudia while I was traveling. It said, "Hi Sis, I hope you are having a great trip."

I was floored. She called me "Sis." She had never called me that before. Not only that, she had never sought me out before. She had never contacted me like that, just to send a sweet wish. We had never talked with any terms of endearment and always just got straight to the point. When I got the "Sis" text I was so touched! My eyes flooded with tears over the tiny gesture she had made.

I knew this was all because of the effort I had put in. I couldn't let our old, stunted relationship be all there was between us. I was very conscious of making time and space for her and I kept doing it until it became second nature for me. I feel like I have won the lottery. Everything I did to build the bridge with her was like buying a lottery ticket and I hit the jackpot.

The word "love" doesn't necessarily make sense when it comes to business relationships, but the concept is still the same. I had a breakdown with my business partner and all I had done about it was complain about him. I knew something was wrong for over a year, but instead of talking to him about it, I complained.

When I finally asked myself, "What is missing here?" I realized it was that I wasn't taking responsibility for my part in it. He was not handling things the way I thought he should and I was walking on eggshells around him and not being real with him at all. I went to him and told him what I needed from him and how I felt about the way things had been going. I also told him what he could expect from me in the future. This made all the difference! He understood my position and our relationship was much smoother from that time onward. I didn't go to him with demands, I just initiated a potentially difficult conversation and I gave him what I wanted him to give me.

Getting to this point absolutely requires going through the stages we have already been going over in this book. It is cathartic. There is no skipping ahead; you can't get to one place without going through another. In order to be ready for this step, you've got to acknowledge your sob stories, and you've got to let people in. You have to stop living Groundhog Day. Understand the lies you're telling yourself. Look at your fears and the communities of people you surround yourself with. Clear up those things so you can be ready for honest and intimate relationships.

I want to be totally upfront in explaining that this shift did not happen because I demanded things from other people. When we want change, we often look outside of ourselves and ask someone else to change. I looked closely at who I was and changed myself based on what I wanted, and as I made those changes everything else improved. This doesn't necessarily happen quickly. It could take a year, or even ten years, but if you are willing to put the effort into changing yourself, you're going to see your life transform.

Even if you are making efforts toward someone who is not responding, being loving and honest will make you feel better. You will create love. Whatever is missing in your life is what you are not putting in. That gives you a lot of room to take action. If you don't feel loved, you are likely not giving love. If you are bored it is probably because you are boring. You can change that. There is so much power from that perspective.

I feel that we are all meant to be in an intimate relationship with another person. Everything I have ever done has been more enjoyable when I am in a relationship with my partner, versus being on my own or with my girlfriends. Now that I am in a healthy relationship, it enhances all parts of my life. Having the right person means there is someone else who supports you and will not accept the lies that you tell yourself. They hold you to a higher standard and they see you in a better light than you can see yourself. Because they see you regularly, they can pull you up when you fall or give you a wake-up call if you need one.

When my current boyfriend, Elbert, opens the car door for me he sometimes speaks into an imaginary lapel speaker and says, "Madame President is exiting the vehicle." It's silly, but it makes me feel special. I take time to do things like cook for him to help him eat healthier so he feels better. We acknowledge one another and it makes us both happier.

This kind of relationship is a bit like living with a mirror. You do for one another and you notice things about them even when they don't see them in themselves. If you find yourself avoiding this kind of intimate relationship there is probably something in your history you should investigate.

As I mentioned in the last chapter, when I hear people complain that there are no good men or women out there, I think, "*Stop telling yourself lies!*" There are really good people out there. If you are attracting undesirable people, it is time for you to become a great person too. To attract great, you have to become great. When I worked on myself I found a better relationship. I became generous, kind, active, and loving. I never demanded that my boyfriend open doors for me, it was his response to the thoughtful things I did for him, like giving him a foot massage or randomly touching his cheek and saying "I love you."

Many of us have an idea of the "perfect mate." Lord knows, there are enough clichés about them. I find that more important than the characteristics of this intangible mate are the characteristics of the relationship you want.

Elbert and I had been seeing each other casually for about five years. We enjoyed one another's company, but I had a clear vision of what I wanted in a relationship and I thought it couldn't be with him. I had a vision of a supportive, compassionate, loyal person who cared for me, but that wasn't him at the time. When I was sick he might call and tell me he hoped I would feel better, but he didn't come by and help me. We were not committed to each other. We weren't in what I consider a relationship.

When I started to work on myself I got serious about what I wanted and I made a list. In addition to the caring mate, my list included someone who wants the finer things in life, who likes my kids, and who supports me in my business. This simple act of getting specific about my desired partner made me look at where I was lacking.

One night, I was at a conference and Elbert came as my guest to visit and support me. We were sitting in a break area of the hotel and I looked at him and I realized in that moment that I could make our relationship grow. I knew it was time to tell him what had been brewing in my mind.

"Elbert, I am ready for us to be more. I want to love you and I want you to love me. I am willing to begin a life with you if you are ready."

That changed everything.

"That's what I want too," he smiled.

It seems a little formal, but we made an agreement that very moment and *that* is when "seeing each other" became a relationship. We made a commitment to be great people together. We didn't get into details. We just became softer and more loving toward one another. We became more sensitive and responsive. There was no going back to inconsequential and vague. We were in it.

This is an ongoing practice. We are always choosing the way we relate to one another. I constantly remind myself that I want to be in this super-powered relationship with him. I am committed to loving him and I give him my time and attention. We make each other better.

Intimacy with my children is something I practice as well. Like most kids, as my daughter grew up, she wasn't as physically affectionate with me. I would try to hold her hand in the car as we always had, and she would pull away. She was about 9 years old the first time she did that and I was really hurt. I got angry and told her she'd be sorry one day when I'm dead and gone. I wanted her love and she rejected me. *Ouch.*

I read a book called *What Shamu Taught Me About Life, Love, and Marriage.* It's behavior modification 101. For 21 days I challenged myself to reach for her hand, in spite of her rejections. I wanted that closeness back in my life. Every day she would snap her hand back as if to say, "Don't touch me!" but I kept on trying. She tried to keep her hand where I couldn't reach it, but I grabbed it anyway. By the ninth day, she reached for *my* hand. I didn't say anything, but I was in shock, like, "Oh my God, this really works!" There was no negative reaction from me during those 21 days when she snapped her hand back. I approached it like "OK. Let's try again tomorrow."

Kids naturally move away from their parents a bit as they grow up, but I want to make sure my kids know how loved they are, so I am making more and more efforts with them as they get older. When I made a list of things that make me happy, the item at the top of the list was talking to my kids every day. It makes us more present in each other's lives. So I asked them to please let me hear from them in some way each day. All of them agreed and it has been about a year now. We talk or at least text daily and it has deepened our relationships so much. It's a small action, but I seek them out and they respond. This has made my kids more present with one another as well.

We attract people at our common level of brokenness or our common level of emotional health. This means that if you want to attract a healthy, loving partner, you need to become that kind of person first. An emotionally healthy person is not going to be attracted to an insecure, needy person. Like attracts like, remember? What needs to happen for you to become healthy enough to attract the relationships you want?

Chapter 15: Why are You Settling When You Could Have it All?

"If you don't know what you want, you'll never find it. If you don't know what you deserve, you'll always settle for less. You will wander aimlessly, uncomfortably numb in your comfort zone, wondering how life has ended up here." - Rob Liano

By now you have taken in a lot. I have presented a lot of ideas and to get to this point, you must have been diligent in learning about clearing up all of the areas of your life. You have trained yourself to notice when you are telling old lies about yourself and the world you live in. With all of the work you have done, you must have seen some shifts in your life. It's incredible, isn't it?

So, what else is possible?

As women, we often hear the expression "having it all." This implies that you can have a fulfilling career, loving and stable relationships, family, a thriving romantic life, money, health, and success. This also conjures up 1980's images of harried mothers in shoulder pads and spiked heels scrambling to get to their kids' soccer games after work. "Having it all" is a mantra that many see as an impossible struggle.

I once heard someone say "You can have it all, just not all at the same time." When I heard that it made sense to me. But it really made me complacent in my life. I thought, "Okay. Right now I'm really happy with my business. My business is going really good. My relationships with my family are not so good, but right now business works, so it's OK. My family relationships will be good at another time." That was a big lie I was telling myself. It allowed me to settle for my life rather than creating the urgency of improving it.

Look at your life and see where you might be settling for less than what you want. Are you having the same conversations over and over? Do you find yourself spending money in unproductive ways that create stress for you later? Where can you make some small changes or even just notice where you have fallen into habits that aren't getting you what you want or where you want to be? Where are you on auto-pilot?

When you aren't happy, why not make yourself happier? Try to find and add what is missing. One thing that struck me as I started to make changes was that I finally had some money in the bank. The first time I saw $7,000 in my account my jaw dropped. I had curbed my spending on items that gave me short-term satisfaction and I had been able to accumulate some savings. I remember thinking, "Wow, if I don't spend money on frivolous things, I can actually keep a cushion of money. Why have I been depriving myself of that feeling of security?"

I was depriving myself of a lot of things that made me feel good. I love my aunts and uncles, but I rarely visited them outside of holidays. I was too busy and I thought, "They know I love them. They're okay." But then I realized I could do much more and we would all benefit. What about just stopping by to visit or consistently calling on Wednesday nights to see how they are? I was not doing those things which added so much to my life. When I gave more time, I got this great feeling, like the kind you get when you go to church or go to the gym. I was creating joy and stronger bonds.

When I talk about "having it all," I mean demanding more from your life. For instance, a few years ago I saw my doctor for a regular checkup and he told me I was a pint low on blood and he could not tell me why. He also said that I was anemic and I had an irregular heartbeat. This health scare had my mind racing. "Maybe I have cancer. Why is my blood low?" When my panic subsided, I focused on working with my health coach and my trainer. I started to see even more value in investing in my health. After four months of eating clean, gluten-free, and cutting out the bad food, I went back to my doctor and he told me everything was normal. All my tests were normal. We were both surprised!

"Do you work out?" the doctor asked.

"No. I don't like to. I get tired right away. It's just not my style."

"You know, being anemic lowers your energy. That's probably why you don't feel good when you work out," he said.

I insisted, "Sometimes I feel like everything goes black when I work out. I'm just not built for it. It's not my thing."

I realized how long I had been saying that line, "It's not my thing." All of my life. As a kid with sports, I had felt that way. I had always been anemic, but I didn't put it together. I always thought, "Well, I'm more of a yoga person," and "I'm more of a golf person versus softball, volleyball ... I'm more low impact," as if it were a matter of taste, not really due to my health issues. It was another lie. Another wakeup call.

When my father died, I learned even more. There were so many things I could've told him that I didn't because I felt uncomfortable about it. I feel I was a good daughter, but like most of us, there is that regret that I could have been different with him. I could have done more. My wakeup call there was that life isn't forever and you need to make time and cherish the moments that you have with family. I had been reviving my family relationships before he died, but I really started to lean into it even more afterward. I don't want to hold back any more.

So we can be motivated to make improvements in our lives in a lot of different ways, but there is no reason to settle when you can have it all. Take an inventory of the different areas of your life and when you see a place where you may be settling or you are unhappy or uncomfortable, ask yourself, "How can I be happier in this area?" or "How could this be more fun or give me more satisfaction?" Scan through your life and look for the places where you can raise the bar because nobody else is going to do that for you.

You have to do this work yourself. You will be the one who is looking forward and thinking about what you want. You get to push the envelope and you can use all the other tools we've gone over so far to help you with that. These ideas are meant to build upon one another and allow you to have it all.

Chapter 16: Be a Millionaire of Time

"You don't build the life you want by saving time. You build the life you want, and then time saves itself. Recognizing that is what makes success possible." - Laura Vanderkam

We are living in interesting times. Busyness is basically a status symbol these days. When we ask someone how they are doing, often times they reply with "busy," "overloaded," "swamped," or "tied up." Remember, your words create your world. I constantly hear people telling themselves the lie that they have no time and people around them nod their heads as if it is a reality. Take responsibility for the words you use. Erase the phrase, "I don't have time," and replace it with, "It's not a priority to me." This can be eye-opening because "I wish I had time to spend with my family," becomes "My family isn't a priority to me." That sounds awful, doesn't it? I have found that changing my perspective, language, and habits has allowed me to have time for everything. I consider myself a "millionaire of time" because I create time for anything I want.

Before I made this realization, I often felt like I had a lack of time, but then I noticed that my mind was racing all the time, even when I sat like a zombie in front of the TV. I was preoccupied and nowhere near present. I wondered and worried about how to grow my business, I replayed conversations in my head. There was nothing productive about it. I wasn't asking myself questions, I wasn't doing anything proactive. There is a big difference between strategically spending time being visionary and obsessively fretting about your life. That is just complaining in your mind.

I also spent a lot of time micromanaging my employees. I would constantly spot-check their work. It was overkill and not the best use of my time, but when I started to see my company succeeding, it was like an affirmation that I was good enough. I became addicted to the work and the need for acknowledgment, which depleted me, rather than filling me up.

If you want to become a millionaire of time, you will need to look at any "addictions" you have because they are probably the biggest time suckers in your life. Whether it is working late hours, watching TV, eating, video gaming, drinking, social media, draining relationships, or any number of other distractions, consider very honestly where you are spending your time. This investigation will pay off and you may be surprised at what you find.

For me, one of the things that really stood out as a time sucker was the phone. I went to a training once where the presenter stated that successful people don't answer their phones. Mine was a major distraction and I had to put some boundaries on it. I love talking to my sisters and friends, but I have set a certain amount of time to complete something, so I don't stay on calls unless they are urgent. I ask to return the call at a better time and get right back to what I was doing. That way, even if it is a business call, I can get back to the person when it is a good time for me and I am prepared and ready to listen. It's also helpful when I have a bit of an agenda for the conversation so that we don't spend too much time on topics that aren't helpful.

I started to look at my time like building blocks. I did an inventory of what was there and I found that while my business was getting lots of time, there was no block for relationships. There were big gaps in my life and I was completely out of balance. Wellness had no space there. Some of the things I claimed were most important to me were given no time, attention, or energy and I realized I wanted to do something about it.

The life I wanted to create did not include staying up all night working. I was living that way because I didn't intentionally create the life I was operating in, I just wandered into it without intention, so my addiction to work and approval took over. What I wanted to create was a business that ran itself while I participated in loving relationships with my family. I wanted to create travel, learning, fun, peace, and abundance.

One of the most valuable tools I use to create this life for myself is delegating. One day I found myself picking up the phone to follow up on a bill, when I had three people in my office who were being paid to do that sort of thing. I caught myself and realized this was me micromanaging and not using my time wisely. I put the phone back down and from that point forward, I recognized my urge to step in where it wasn't necessary and I was able to stop myself. I find that like most things, delegating takes practice. You have to train yourself to step back and trust that you do not need to handle everything yourself. It takes some discipline and willpower. Today, I find myself free of wanting to jump in and do things that aren't my work! Trusting that everything will be handled without my double-checking and butting in gives me time for my priorities. *Freedom!*

Delegating isn't just about work. Asking your husband/wife, kids, friends, significant other, or family for help is just as valuable. Allow them to help you. If you have a long list of things to handle and you are getting overwhelmed, someone else can put gas in your car or go to the market just as well as you can. Don't insist on taking on everything. As women, we are conditioned to be caregivers and sometimes we don't let people help us because we are convinced that we do things better or faster, and we don't want to let go of control. That kind of control is settling for less and will never allow you to have it all, not to mention all the time it takes away from you.

The other big benefit to delegating is that it gives you another opportunity to appreciate the people in your life. Saying, "Thank you so much for helping me. What you did for me allowed me to be so much more productive today," will strengthen your relationships even more. Everyone wins! By all means, don't delegate things that you really enjoy, but millionaires of time ask for help and take it.

You have the same 24 hours per day that Mother Teresa and Einstein had. Look at what they were able to accomplish. Oprah doesn't get more time in her day than you do. The key is to use your time in a way that gets you what you want. Be intentional, even in your down time. Allow for free time, but don't fritter it away fussing over things that need to be done! Make space for greater possibilities as you move through the miracles we are creating here.

Take your time; it is *yours*.

Chapter 17: Sibling Rivalry, My Hidden Agenda, and Four Visits with Rosie

"A sister is both your mirror – and your opposite." – Elizabeth Fishel

I read a quote from Margaret Mead once, "Sister is probably the most competitive relationship within the family, but once the sisters are grown, it becomes the strongest relationship." I know this is true for many families, but I think especially families who grow up in lack. There is never enough of anything and you have to grab what you can for yourself or you won't get anything at all. It becomes an "every man for himself" coping strategy.

Just because my family is of critical importance to me doesn't mean we always have the easiest time communicating. My sister, Rosie has been living in Texas for several years with her husband and son. The first time I went to visit her I came with my sister Brenda, my brothers Jesse and Adrian, and my daughter Frances. The kids were little, between 8-12 years old. We went to a mall together. While the kids saw a movie, Rosie, Brenda, and I went to a restaurant to catch up. Rosie took out a flask and poured vodka into her drink while we were waiting for the waiter to bring our food. Rosie drinks like that. She usually carries a Big Gulp cup with alcohol in it and wears really big, Jackie Onassis-type sunglasses so that you can't see that she's drunk.

We met the kids after the movie and Rosie insisted on driving us all home. When I told her I should drive because she had been drinking she became furious and we began to argue in the parking lot. Then she got in her car and took off without us. All of a sudden, she threw the car into reverse and sped back to where we were, as if she was going to run us over. We all jumped out of the way to avoid being hit and she slammed on the breaks.

"Get the fuck in!" she ordered.

"Hell no!" I said, shocked.

"Well then, fuck you," and she flew off in the car again, leaving us there.

There we were, stranded in a Texas shopping mall parking lot. We didn't have her address. All of our things were at her house. I called her husband and he picked us up. When we got back to her apartment she was drinking heavily. Her boss happened to be there and he and her son and husband faded into the background.

"Look," she sneered, "that's them, the conceited bitches. They came all the way from L.A. to go sightseeing. Not to see me, but to go sightseeing."

I told the kids to gather up their things and we'd go somewhere until she calmed down.

"Get the fuck out of here! Just get the fuck out of here!" Rosie bellowed.

While we were getting our luggage together she started throwing things at us.

"Oh, you forgot your shoes!" A shoe came flying my way.

She picked up a small suitcase and was about to fling it when my sister Brenda turned on her.

"You better not, Rosie. You need to stop it right there because I'm not just going to stand here and take it," Brenda said calmly, but seriously.

Rosie dropped the bag at her feet and we left the apartment.

After the door closed behind us, Rosie's boss told her, "Hey, relax. That's your family." Rosie grabbed a heavy snow globe and hurled it at his head. He ducked out of the way and it smashed on the wall behind him, barely missing him.

"Rosie, you're fired."

He left the apartment and found us walking down the street with our luggage. There was no Uber then and we didn't know where to find a taxi in this private neighborhood. He helped us find a hotel and we stayed there until she called me and told me she regretted her actions. We went back to her place after she promised she wouldn't drink, but after the chaos of the first day it was awkward.

When I started doing personal development and finding out what I do that allows drama in my life, I had to look at how I was shaping my kids. I'm teaching them how to deal with situations. I also realized that I could have reacted differently when we were in Texas. I didn't have to get angry. I could have ridden the wave and not fed the drama. I didn't have to let that night result in being kicked out of Rosie's house. She loves me, I love her, and we had gone all the way to Texas. By insisting that we got to a hotel I probably made things worse. I didn't return to visit her again until seven years later.

I never stopped communicating with Rosie. I missed her. She calls me when she's drunk and she cries. Some people in the family won't speak to her. She causes a lot of drama. If you confide something in her, she'll tell your secrets. When she's drunk she'll tell people what you've said in confidence. I want to keep talking to her. I want relationships that work. So when I returned to Texas for a second time, I set an intention before I got there. "No matter what happens, if she kicks me out, I'm not leaving."

I took my daughter and my brother. This time my daughter was 17 and my brother was 19. Rosie and I were hanging out in her room talking. I approached her about her drinking, and how it's going to impact her son in the future.

"Oh, he's so little that ... he's fine," she waved me off.

"Rosie, it's very likely he's going to need therapy from all he's seen."

"So you're telling me I'm fucking up my son?" I could feel the volume turning up on the situation.

"What I'm saying is, it is probable that he will need therapy."

"*So you're saying I'm fucking up my son,*" she repeated. "You know what? Get the fuck out of my house. Get the fuck out of my house!"

My brother told me he heard this from another room and thought "Here we go again..." We hadn't even been there for four hours yet. But I had set the intention that I wasn't leaving.

"I'm sorry. I don't mean to upset you. I don't want to leave. I came here to see you. I love you." I just softened it up, and we got beyond it. So I stayed and it was a really nice visit, even though she drank the entire time.

Regardless, I got to spend some good time with Rosie and her family. They really love each other, and they have a rhythm of making it work around her drinking. They normalize it.

Around this time, my mom had gone missing again. It had been four months since anyone in the family had seen her. She called once in a while and her voice was so weak, it was clear she was not doing well. She didn't tell us where she was, she didn't want us to see her. When she got out of prison, she was 62 years old and was released to Mexico, not the U.S. because she was undocumented. I set her up in an apartment and I visited her as much as I could but she was lonely in Mexico. She hadn't called it home since she was 9 years old. She had no friends and only one estranged brother. She became depressed and stopped taking her many medications. She was soon diagnosed with severe depression and abandonment syndrome by a psychologist. She lost over 40 pounds rapidly and seemed disoriented most of the time. I did everything I could think of but she just didn't know how to function in the regular world after prison.

I was alone and on my way to see Rosie about a year after my previous visit. I was going to a training, which I specifically chose because it was close to her in Houston. Between connecting flights I picked up a message from my brother telling me something awful had happened. My mother had died from a heart attack.

It was terrible news, but not entirely unexpected, given her circumstances. It had been such a long odyssey with my mother.

My family was together at home in L.A. gathering to support one another. Rosie is all alone in Texas as far as family goes, so the timing was perfect because we could be together. I ended up being the one to give her the news about my mom. When I called Rosie she said, "Come. Come here now."

I went to her and she was really strong. She helped me a lot, knowing how I felt about my mom. Rosie hadn't seen my mom in 14 years. But later she started to fall apart, blaming herself for not making more time and not being a better daughter. For the next three days we were together, supporting each other. It was really beautiful and I'm so grateful that I happened to be close to her when our mother died and we were feeling such loss. We drank together—got drunk together. She cooked a lot of food and really hosted me. It was a loving and caring experience and we bonded closer than ever.

I was thinking back over that time recently and I had a big breakthrough about how I behave around my sisters. I desperately want their love and approval. My sister Brenda had told me once that it seemed like I was bragging when I was telling her about some success I had had. I had to think about that, but no. There is no piece of me that wants anyone to feel badly because I am doing well. The reality is that when I tell my sisters about significant things in my life I am really saying *love me. Approve of me. Let me know that I am doing well.* I had no idea that I needed that so much, nor how it was being received by them. I was completely blind to it.

I took a class where the presenter said, "Consider that we all have hidden agendas, and our job is to find out what they are." The work is to find out *why you do what you do.* If you can't think of anything, keep thinking. I thought my brain was going to explode! I couldn't think of a thing. Then I made the connection with Brenda's comment about me bragging. I realized that every time I talked to my sisters, afterward I felt a kind of inauthenticity. As if I wasn't present. It didn't feel easy. It was always a heavy effort with them.

Once I made that connection there was no going back. That was my hidden agenda. I realized that I am always trying to get them to show me their love and approval. I have to remember that they love me no matter what. At ground zero they love me for me. Now I look back and realize, just like all the money I wasted on bounced checks, how much energy I wasted on vying for their love and approval, which I had all along! Now that I understand, I feel so free. I feel like I'm not even touching the ground.

I set on a mission to spend more time with each of my sisters and to let them know how much I love them. Knowing this hidden agenda of mine has made me more conscious of being authentic and present with them. To begin with I sent them a post on social media about sisterly love, just a little thing so they would know I was thinking about them lovingly. I reach out to them more regularly and make the focus that I love them rather than just giving them an update on what I am doing in my life. (Although, it now occurs to me that it might still be part of my hidden agenda. Maybe I am trying to make them love me by sending them love notes. Those damn agendas get sneakier the more we unearth them...)

I took Jeanette to Vegas a few times, once with her family and once just the two of us. It was such fun to vacation together and not worry about anything. I also hired her to do some work for me that wasn't really important, but it meant that she would come to my home and stay overnight and give her a little respite and getaway.

I had a harder time making plans with Claudia. She didn't seem able to make any time for us, so I created a situation where she would have to see me to sign a paper. I came to her office and while I was there her boss asked her to lunch and I joined the group. She seemed happy about that. I think her hidden agenda was that I might impress her boss. It wasn't just the two of us, as I would have liked, but I was happy for her. She looked so beautiful and I could finally focus on her rather than wondering what she thought about me.

When I talked to Brenda I had been journaling about her for a while. I invited her to dinner and I made it a really lovely night for the two of us. She was my first houseguest in my new home. I was nervous while trying to make it special. I cooked a healthy meal, bought new towels, gave her flowers, and really tried to set the stage for showing her how important she is to me and how I want to work on our relationship.

When Rosie came to Los Angeles for my mother's funeral services, I booked her a two-day turnaround on the flight because my family was nervous about her being in California. It is a toxic environment for her. Thirteen years before this, we had to trick her into moving to Texas. She needed to get away from the people and the drugs in L.A. Back then her father was sick and needed to see her so we bought her a one-way ticket to Texas. When Rosie called Claudia saying that she was ready to come back to California, Claudia told her, "I'm not gonna give you the ticket to come back. I think you need to stay over there." So Rosie ended up staying, but she and Claudia no longer speak. Even though she still has addiction issues, Texas is a better place for her.

When Rosie came back for our mother's funeral, she complained that her visit was too short.

"Why did you get the ticket for only two days? We could've stayed the whole week," she said.

But that was it, two days was all I gave her. She and her husband still mention how short that trip was for them. I haven't confessed that it was planned that way, though now that I think about it, I know I should ... OK, I will. I am living in truth, so I must.

It had been two years since I had visited Rosie and I had been traveling lot. She complained that I hadn't been to see her. Her husband took the phone from her when we were talking one night.

"Are you gonna come and see her before she dies? The way she is living, you better hurry or you'll miss your chance. She won't last long. Your sister will be dead soon."

I believed him. I don't know all of the details but I know my sister has pain in her stomach and a growth under her arm. She doesn't take care of herself. She went to the dentist and they told her that her liver problems are manifesting in her teeth. Apparently that is common with Cirrhosis patients. I don't know if she has Cirrhosis, but it would make sense. Also she drinks and drives. I had known things were bad, but I saw that it was a really big deal when her husband took the phone from her that day. He never does things like that with me. He was warning me that I might never see her again, so I made my plans for a fourth visit to see Rosie.

I was strategic about my arrival. I came in late at night and took a cab to her house, knowing she'd be passed out when I got there. I wanted a fresh start with her, and she doesn't start drinking in the morning, so I knew I would have a window of time with her being focused. (Much like my mother would be in bed when her drunk boyfriend came home so he wouldn't start in on her, I knew how to avoid seeing Rosie at a prime time for drunken drama.) Her son took the day off from school and we all went to breakfast. We rented a movie, we laughed, and we caught up.

It just so happened that I got some huge news about my business during this visit. I had set a goal of getting 500 referrals and I had been stuck at 300 for a long time. It seemed like 500 was an impossible number to reach. While Rosie and I were hanging out one night I got a text from my office.

"Oh my God, Rosie," I gasped. "A miracle just happened. I just hit 500 referrals in my business!"

"What does that mean?"

I started to explain and I could see that she didn't fully understand, but she knew it was a big deal for me and she got excited with me.

"You know what? I always have wondered where I would be when I got this news, so I'm going to make a little video," I told her.

I didn't expect her to be in the video, but before I knew it she was jumping up and down chanting "500! 500! 500!" She was in the background of the video with her Big Gulp cup, cheering for me. I really felt that she was happy for me. It didn't matter that she wasn't quite clear on what we were celebrating. There was nothing for her to gain in that moment, but there was nothing taken from her either. I can't remember the last time I saw her happy and jumping up and down like that.

It was a night of celebrating. We played dress up in her closet. Faux fur coats, high heels, jewelry, bags, hats, and even a tutu! We were giddy and silly and it was wonderful. We danced around, sang songs, made videos and sent them to the family. It was a whole new way of being together for us. Again, I was grateful to be with her when big news hit.

In making these efforts with my sisters, I have noticed that they are more receptive to me. They are softer toward me. I'll never be able to control what my sisters do, but I can control my reaction and the way I approach them. I love them openly and they love me back.

A hidden agenda is an oblique plan designed to accomplish, change, fix, destroy, remedy, reward, punish, promote or hinder something we want. We all have them. Can you find your own hidden agenda? Is there something you do or a way that you act that is really an ulterior motive for some kind of personal gain? Think hard. Who is the person you do this with? What do you want from them that you aren't getting? Why do you want or need it? Again, start small and find that awareness.

Part 3: Mastering the Miracles

Chapter 18: Where do You See Yourself in Five Years?

"You cannot change your destination overnight. You can change your direction." - Jim Rohn

With the question, "Where do you see yourself in 5 years?" I do not mean for you to answer as if you are in your millionth lame, corporate job interview. I want you to challenge yourself to construct an answer that feels real and true for you. List what is important so you can zero in on what you want.

Wishes are weak, but wants are potent. To me, wishing is wasteful. There is no action behind it. Wishes don't come from a place of power. I often hear people wistfully say how they wish they could do or have something in their life, as if they'll never get what they want unless a magic genie comes to them and grants them their wish. You don't get what you wish for, you get what you work for.

Here is the difference: A *wish* is, "I wish I weighed 20 pounds less," but with no action to make it happen. If you aren't going to do anything about it, it's really just another way of complaining. A *want* is, "I am ready to lose weight," and finding a trainer, committing to a morning walk, keeping unhealthy food out of your home, building a support system with friends, and being accountable for how you will get what you want. Embrace the emotion and motivation and you will move forward.

I am part of a women's group where we envision the future and answer questions about what it will take to get from here to there. I remember being asked to look at my future self. What do you look like? Where are you? I saw myself as a version of Sigourney Weaver. About 60 years old, wearing a powerful suit in a beautiful office. She exuded confidence and strong sense of self. We were asked what advice we would give our current self and all I could think was, "It's going to be OK." That gave me so much peace and took away a lot of angst. Now I see myself the way I saw her. I have already reached that vision. I am a strong, confident, successful woman.

If I had never gone through that exercise, I would not have had the clarity of what I wanted. Taking the time to get to know yourself and what you want isn't self-indulgent; it is imperative to create the map to follow for the life you want to live. It can be a small shift in thinking that opens massive possibility for you. When you feel stuck in a situation it is hard to imagine getting what you want. When you feel like a powerless victim to life, things like travel, relationships, and money may seem untouchable. I hope that the ideas in the previous chapters are empowering you to see a future because you can't create something you can't see.

Things were really opening up between Rosie and me and on that fourth visit she pulled me aside.

"I'd like for you to spend time one-on-one with my son, because I think that he doesn't like school. I want you to talk to him to find out if he's being bullied."

I agreed and she went to the market. Her son had told me that he likes time travel books, so I thought this might be a good place to start.

"You know how to tell the future, right?" I asked.

"No. How do you do that?"

"You create it. The best way to know the future is to create it. Do you want to create the future?"

We each took out a large sheet of white paper, so I could play alongside him.

"Okay, you're 11 years old today. 20 years from now, where are you? Are you married? Do you have kids?"

He said, "Yes, I'm married. I have two kids."

"How old are you?"

"31."

"Okay. What's your occupation?"

"I'm gonna be a famous basketball player," and he drew it on the sheet of paper.

"What kind of house are you going to live in?" I asked.

"I'm gonna live in a mansion," and he drew a very detailed mansion with 25 windows. He's a really good artist like his mom.

Then I asked, "What kind of car are you gonna have?"

"A G-Wagon, and my wife is gonna have a convertible pink car," and he drew that.

"What are you going to do with all that money? How are you gonna spend it?"

He said, "I'm gonna take my kids to soccer. I'm gonna take my kids skiing. I'm gonna be on vacation with my kids."

"How much money are you going to make?"

"A gazillion dollars," and he drew all the zeros. He drew a one with a hundred zeros

.

"Okay. Well, that's all fine and great when you're successful, but anybody who is successful works hard, so why don't we go forward in the future just 10 years from now. What are you gonna be doing to prepare yourself for that future? In 10 years how old are you?"

"21."

"What are you doing?"

"I'm in college."

"Which college?"

He said, "Rice University, it's in Houston."

"Draw that."

"I don't know how to draw it, because I don't know what it looks like."

So we got a picture from the internet, and he looked at it for a second, and drew it like a copy of it. Then he drew himself playing basketball on the team at college. He drew the bleachers, the scoreboard, everything. He said that he was going to be dating, and he drew himself on dates; having dinner, going to the movies, and hanging out. He drew himself playing basketball with his friends. It was so good to see him opening up to ideas like that.

So then when my sister arrived we showed her what we were working on.

"Mom, you gotta do it too!"

She agreed and I began the same way with her.

"Okay. Let's go into the future and see the future you can create. In 10 years from now where are you going to be?"

She drew a headstone.

"Rosie, stop."

"No, really. I don't see myself here in 10 years. I'm gonna be dead. You know, Hazel, since I was 19 I have been wanting to kill myself. Every day I do something that kills me, something that's gonna kill me eventually. I don't know why, but I don't want to be here. I don't want to be alive. And I drink, and I've done drugs, because I want to kill myself slowly. Because I believe that if I commit suicide God's gonna be mad at me. So I've been killing myself slowly and I don't think I'm gonna be around in 10 years. I know I could go to therapy and probably get some medicine, but I don't want to. What I really want is to die. The only reason I haven't died yet, is because of my son. All I've been doing is waiting for him to be ready to be without me. I know I'm fucked up and I'm giving him a bad example by drinking. But I think at least he still has me. If it was not for him, I wouldn't be here right now."

She was crying as she said all this. She had never said things like that to me. She has scars from cutting her wrists. I knew, but I didn't know. She was holding all of that inside of her and I had been so focused on getting her approval that I wasn't able to see her clearly and be a safe, open person for her. I was so honored that she trusted me and told me her truth.

"All right, Sis. Well, let's do this thing. Why don't we create the best case scenario, and not the worst case scenario? The best case scenario is you are around in 10 years. What would it be?"

"I would own this house that we live in. We rent and I really like this house. I don't want to move. I want to die in this house," she said as if she had just thought of it.

"Okay, draw the house."

So she drew the house and she drew it beautifully. She added flowers and all sorts of lovely details.

Then she drew herself with a fit, healthy body. She drew herself in love with her husband, together in love with him. She drew her son with a cap and gown.

"How much money are you going to be making?"

"I'm gonna be making so much money that I'm not gonna work anymore. I'm gonna be living off of one of my inventions." Rosie has a lot of cool ideas and invents smart things, but then she doesn't follow through.

She was getting into the exercise and then she got oddly quiet. She gave me a hug, and she told me, "You make me want to live. I can't believe this. This is literally the first time that I actually could see my future."

After I had returned home I got a text from her.

For as long as I can remember I have been talking to my son about how I'm gonna die one day and preparing him for where he's gonna go and the people he can count on in life, and you're one of them. I've always told him, Hazel's gonna be there for you. If something happens to me, she's gonna take care of you. Today I had a talk with him, and I told him, guess what? I'm not gonna die after all, and he better prepare for me being an old lady and in his life.

It was another absolute miracle. This beautiful, broken woman whom I love so much has not seen a future for herself since she was 19 years old. When she used her ability to see her future, there was hope again. Every time I think of that visit my heart brims over with love and appreciation for her.

Look at the areas of your life and ask yourself what you want to see 5 years from now. When you answer these questions, answer with the perfect outcome, no limitations. Don't be scared to go big! Write down your answers without any consideration of price.

How do you want your body and mind to feel?

How much money do you want to have in the bank?

Where do you want to go on vacation?

Where do you want to live?

What career do you want?

When I did this exercise, I was making about $4,000 per month. I wrote that I wanted a pimped-out mansion, I wanted to drive a Porsche, I wanted to be a semi-professional golfer, I wanted to travel around the world first-class, and I wanted fancy dinners, a personal trainer, and a fit body.

The next step of the exercise is to go back and look at how much the things on your list cost. I had to do some homework. I found a house that seemed like my ideal, which cost one million dollars. The Porsche I wanted was $80,000. Golf lessons were $140 per hour, so then I needed to know how many times I wanted to take lessons each week and multiply by that number. I broke it all down so it was more bite-sized. I didn't have to be a millionaire to have these things. This made it all so much less scary. The house may cost one million dollars, but the payments are $5,000. I didn't have the $80,000 for the car, but the monthly payment for that was $650. This process made the things I wanted much more real. Of course I was still only making $4,000, so it wasn't like I could make it all happen that instant, but just breaking it down made it seem more attainable.

Then I started doing the things that were available to me in that moment. I test drove the Porsche I liked. I went to open houses. I met with a golf teacher and I was able to afford a personal trainer. I started shifting where I was spending my money so I could have some of the things I really wanted. I was able to actively work toward that.

I realized that I was going to have to make ten times what I was making to live the lifestyle I desired. What would that take? I had to have a certain number of clients. I had to put out a certain amount of effort to create that. So it became a game plan. Then I had a reason to make more money instead of just a nebulous, wish for it. I had a strategy, an intention, and a place to apply my energy.

I recently bought a new house—or I guess I should be honest and call it a mansion. It has seven bathrooms, four living rooms, a swimming pool, and a Jacuzzi. This is my first house that has a swimming pool. Nobody in my family has ever had a swimming pool. I have over three acres of property with orange trees, grapefruit trees, and pomegranate as well. The best part about this house is the view. I can see all the way to Catalina Island. I can see downtown L.A. I can see Orange County. And every night, I see the Disneyland fireworks. It's remarkable. I mean, it really takes your breath away, the view itself.

This is something I could never have begun to imagine while I was struggling and bouncing checks left and right. This is something I found as I found myself. I worked and discovered what I could do and what I wanted. Then I found the paths and small actions to get me where I am now. My dreams got a little bigger and a little bigger, but it all stemmed from working on myself, getting very honest, and seeing the miracles that appeared.

Think about what it would take to get what you most desire. If it is money you need, think about training for a more lucrative career or a promotion. If you want close, loving relationships, what needs to happen for you to become healthy enough to attract the love of your life? Healthy, loving people attract other healthy, loving people which create the relationships you are craving.

Chapter 19: Become Great

"If you hang out with chickens, you're going to cluck and if you hang out with eagles, you're going to fly." - Dr. Steve Maraboli

Now that you know what you want and have identified some of what it will take to get there, let's look at a way we can speed it up. Whether you want a wonderful partner, great friends, an amazing job, a lovely home, a nice holiday, or a healthier mind and body, it all starts with the person in the mirror—you.

Stop the endless searching. Work to become the person of your dreams first. Everything else will follow. Contribute to what you want. Learn all you can about what you want and apply what you learn to your life immediately. Learn how you can give what you want in order to receive it, because like attracts like. As I have said before, if you are looking for love, be more loving. Be more of what you want. I invite you to think about your own greatness and how and why you should receive what you want. Are you currently worthy of it?

When I say "worthy," it is not to induce judgement upon yourself. Worthiness is not about shame and guilt. It is about knowing whether you are doing your part to attract the things you want. They will not come from fate, luck, or destiny and if they do, you will not keep them long. Be it love, money or status; no one else can produce a better life for you. Challenge yourself to see where you can be doing more, learning more, practicing more, and putting more energy into your endeavors.

When I was out with that group of ladies who were talking about there being "no good men out there," I couldn't help but think, "What are you doing to make yourself worthy of a good man? Are you continually growing as a person? Are you following your dreams? What do you have to offer in this equation?"

When I was visiting the Vatican a few years ago, I stood in complete awe of the beauty of the place, but I also had a feeling of not being worthy of it. There were so many people who were nobler, more deserving, and more in need. When a pastor asked if he could bless me, I nodded, but throughout the blessing I was thinking I didn't deserve it. It was crazy. I am a daughter of God, of course I am worthy! Back in my home life I was operating this way too. I didn't ask people for help often because I didn't want to bother them. I didn't want to look weak by asking for help.

So when you ask yourself if you are worthy of the life you want, ask with love. The answer may be yes, but you may find that in all honesty, you are not doing all you could be doing right now. Think how things would look if you were to contribute more to the greatness of your life.

Whether you feel worthy or not, you can definitely get there. You just need to get busy and be in a state of action. Once I had decided that I wanted to become a money magnet and have money to do whatever I wanted, I shared that desire with a friend who introduced me to a wonderful CPA who handles her money (this friend was already a millionaire). The CPA gave me great advice. I also picked up a book about money and I went to the bank to learn about which kinds of accounts would give me the highest percentage of return on the money I planned to have one day. I got really busy and immersed myself, focusing on wealth. I put energy into what I wanted, I didn't just wait for it to arrive. I watched the money I had as it grew. The big money was still far away, but I was ready for it.

During the collapse of the real estate market in 2007, the value of my house dropped and my business slowed down. I got behind in my house payments and I didn't catch up for five years, so my credit rating suffered. I was in the 500 range and it felt like a deep, dark hole that I would be in forever. It was a matter of integrity to me to figure it out, so that became my focus. I opened an account with Experian and found out exactly what my score was. I paid someone to help me clean up my credit history and raise my score. He taught me what to do to keep it from dropping again and keep a high score. Did you know a high balance on credit cards negatively impact credit scores even if you are paying on time each month? The best thing to do is keep your balance under 30% of the credit line amount. Information like this was foreign to me but I got excited to see my score improve and I monitored my credit daily. Shortly after this I was able to buy a building, a new home, and to lower all of my interest rates. I made more money by fixing my credit.

This may sound odd, but go with me here: If an alien was watching you, a creature with no language, they would only know what was important to you by seeing your actions. What would an alien see you working toward? This question is a great way to recognize if you really are in action.

For example, if I was with my daughter, the alien would see me give her my full attention. He would see me smile and hug her. When the alien saw me at the gym, stretching at home, walking my dogs, going to doctor visits, and cooking and eating healthy food, he would know that my health is a priority to me. He would see me spending time with my sisters and being present with them and recognize my love for my family. These are areas where I am clearly in action and working toward getting what I want.

One more rule I have for myself is "Always be up to something." I find it interesting that when I ask people what is happening with them, I often get the answer, "Same old, same old." That bums me out. I have another set of people in my life who always have lots going on. They are eager to share what is happening in their lives and what they are creating. They are planning a party, working on a book, remodeling their homes, planning a vacation, etc. This is how I live because it is where I am happiest. I keep a "Top 10" list of what I have going on, so when someone asks what is happening with me, I can say, "Do you want the whole list or just the top 10?"

The point is, you can talk until the cows come home, but your words are meaningless without action. Look at what is on your calendar. How does that reflect your goals? Where are you spending your time? Are you giving time and energy to what you want? Wishing and talking won't get you anywhere, so get into action. Put energy into what you want. Educate yourself. Start moving toward what you want, no matter how small your steps are. You have one life. Make it the best.

Chapter 20: If You Say You Want it Easy, Why Are You Making it Hard?

"Life is not complicated. We are complicated. When we stop doing the wrong things and start doing the right things, life is simple." - Angel Chernoff

Easy. Who doesn't want things to be easy in life? Doing the things that can make reaching your goals easier takes attention and energy. If you have a disagreement with your partner, rather than giving in or fighting to the death, just stop the disagreement by acknowledging the other person's point of view. You don't have to change that person's mind or change the argument, you can choose to end the discussion. Be a bit more easygoing to gain the ease you want in life while still moving toward what you want.

I was forever without money in my former life. I would spend money on shoes, movies, and frequently ate in restaurants, so I couldn't save any money and I was always living in lack. Opportunities came and went without me because I didn't have any money saved. I'd drop $150 taking my kids out to eat, when everyone would have been just as happy taking sandwiches to the park for a fraction of that amount. I wanted money to be easy, but I made it harder for myself by overspending on things that didn't matter. I could never say yes to anything big because I frittered away all my money. I lived in a big world full of no, and it was my choices that created it.

If you go back to the list you made in the last chapter with what you want and where you see yourself in 5 years, look at where you are making things harder to achieve. If you want to lose weight, are you eating and exercising in a way that will get you there? How can you make it easier to get what you want? Go through each of the items on the list and see if you are sabotaging yourself with actions that oppose your goals. How can you make it easier to get what you want? Find at least one thing for each item that would help you get there.

I hear people say, "I want to go on vacation, but I don't have any money." They are already saying that the vacation won't happen with that "but." When you want to create something, you can't close the loop like that. "I want to go on vacation," is a complete sentence. Leave it there. Buying into thoughts like "losing weight is hard," will ensure that you don't succeed. It's another lie you are telling yourself. You won't lose weight if you believe it is hard.

An older client who is attending college came to see me the other day and told me how hard school is for her. She's tired compared to the younger kids in the class. She thinks they can do better than she can. I stopped her and said, "Wow, that's a lot of lies you are telling yourself." She was shocked. "You haven't given yourself a chance. Anything worth doing is challenging. It's not hard, it's *challenging*. You need to change your ideas about how you approach school. Get your family to buy into it. Tests are hard when you aren't ready for them. Are you giving yourself the time to study so the test can be easy? Are you making it easy for yourself to get what you say you want?"

Don't justify why you can't do things. That just makes things harder for you. Look for ways that you can make things easier, tiny, minute things. If you are going someplace where parking is difficult, give yourself a little extra time. It's easier to have difficult conversations about delicate topics if you are understanding, empathetic, and compassionate. It doesn't take much to create more ease in your life.

Think about your energy level. I hear people say that they have no energy, but in reality, energy is something you generate. It's like a car battery that recharges as the car runs. We create the energy. When you feel depleted, create the energy to go hiking, or create the energy to make love. Create the energy to get outdoors and walk on the beach.

This is again, creating and visioning your future. Be very careful of disempowering words. You get to create the environment, so create a world full of yes!

VIP RESOURCE:

Visit www.themasteryofmiracles.com/vip-resources to download a free worksheet and guided audio to take you through the Mastery of Miracles visioning process.

Chapter 21: Get Right With Your Source

"You don't choose your family. They are God's gift to you, as you are to them." - Desmond Tutu

By now you know that my family is very important to me. If I acted the way I felt, I would throw rose petals under their feet as they walked. It took me some time to get right with them, but I would have done it years earlier if I had known what I know now. My family is my source. What I mean by source is they make me feel most like myself. They make me part of something much bigger than myself and what it truly means to be a human being. We are much more powerful together with incredible creative potential. They are a source of energy that powers me up with love.

We are all born into families. We don't get to choose one another, and sometimes we don't like each other, yet we are still thrown together. We have different personalities and different ways of handling problems. Mothers, fathers, children, and other immediate family like cousins all gravitate toward one another. We are born knowing that we belong to a family. It's a significant part of who we are to the core. Research has shown that when chimpanzees are born, they immediately seek out their mothers. They have never met their mothers, but they know intrinsically that there is supposed to be a mother there. Like them, we are born knowing that we are meant to belong to something bigger than we are.

At one of the seminars I attended years ago, the speaker said, "If you are not right with the source of your life, you are never going to find the love of your life."

I raised my hand to challenge this, "I don't understand. I am currently not speaking to my sister, my cousin, or my uncle. How is that going to keep me from finding the love of my life?"

I didn't see the connection at all. I didn't think my bad blood with them was stopping me from anything.

The speaker walked off the stage and approached me directly.

"Oh, that doesn't affect you at all?" she asked.

"No. They don't talk to me. I don't like it, but that's okay," I replied.

"So you're fine not talking to your sister," she said, "Tell me about her."

I was crying before I even got the first sentence out. Of course it wasn't fine that I didn't have my sister in my life! I began to realize how important she was and how much I missed her as well as how much I missed my cousin and my uncle. I started to see that if they were in my life it would be so much better. We would all be so much better.

The other thing I realized is how I had built up walls so I could feel okay about them rejecting me. Those walls protected me from the pain of missing my family. I was keeping the pain out, but it also made me numb. I kept out love. Protecting myself prevented me from loving anyone fully. That is what the speaker meant by saying I would never find the love of my life. If I can't love fully, I'll find others who can't love fully either.

I thought that if I cut my family out of my life or claimed that it didn't matter that they stopped talking to me, they couldn't hurt me. Approaching relationships like this means that you miss out on the vulnerable joy in love. Also, people are intricately connected and blocking off one relationship usually affects another. The family outside of myself, my sister, my cousin, and my uncle also suffered because of those rifts. The pain factor was high on all counts.

That changed everything for me. I felt like I was an armadillo that had cracked its shell. The armor I had built to keep away the pain, kept everything good out too, and I was done with that. Every day after that I did something toward having my sister back in my life. I got busy and put energy into it.

When the walls came down, I received a rush of love, and it was reciprocated. With those walls, I blocked myself from love and from money too. Money came like a tidal wave after I finally got right with my family. Once those walls were blown down, I was present and authentic. I began to be more purposeful and to believe in myself. All of my relationships began to work on all four cylinders and I was unstoppable. I broke up with a dramatic business partner who was stunting our growth. When I opened my own business without her, I became much more successful. Many more clients came in and it was all for me. I made all the money decisions in the business and I was good at it. My entire experience of living shifted. My confidence returned and miracles awoke.

My father floated in and out throughout out my life, but after he went to rehab he spent a lot of time with me and my kids. He contributed to the family and that meant so much to me. He worked and he was going to college taking drug and alcohol counseling classes. He helped me with raising my brothers. He would come to holidays and family dinners and he would come to see the kids' sports events. It was a beautiful time. It was what I had always wanted from him and he was finally willing and able to participate in family.

As part of his rehab, he would go back for meetings and maintenance after the main program was over. He met a woman named Amanda there and began seeing her. I think the idea of entering into a relationship with someone you meet in rehab is generally considered a terrible idea. There is a lot to learn about living life sober, and jumping into a relationship with someone who needs to learn these same lessons can make it easy to backslide. He confided in me that he was under a lot of stress because he was not making much money and he was expected to support himself and Amanda as well. The stress led to drinking, which led to crack, and then methadone. After 5 years of sobriety, he surrendered to his addiction.

 Of course there was nothing I could do to make him stop. He knew I loved him and I still saw him on holidays, but it wasn't ever the same again. He would call sometimes, but he would usually be high and he didn't make any sense.

I got a call from a very upset Amanda one day telling me that my father was in the hospital with pneumonia. It had been a few months since I had seen him for his birthday. He was still using drugs heavily. His own mother died not long before and he was too out of it to attend the funeral. When I went to see him to tell him his mother had died he had almost no reaction. He was just flat.

"Dad!" I said "What's wrong with you? Your mom died and you don't even have a response? You are in bad shape. You're going to die if you keep on like this. You need to go back to rehab."

"I'll go," he said. "Will you pay for Amanda to go too?"

"No Dad. I'm not paying for her."

It bothered me a lot that he would ask me to pay for her. I know he's responsible for his own actions, but part of the stress that got him drinking again was having to take care of her. That was not my job.

"Okay, Hazel. I'll register myself and have them call you to make a payment."

But he never went.

And so when he got pneumonia I went to the hospital to see him. He was on a ventilator. He was so thin. The methadone took away his appetite, so he rarely ate. He was this shell of a man. My father.

The doctor told me that he had done a lot of damage to his body over the years and that it would be very difficult for him to recover from the pneumonia. He had been an addict since he was 16 years old. The drugs and hard living had taken their toll and his body could not fight back.

The next day I got a call while I was in a sales meeting telling me that I needed to get back to the hospital right away. I called my aunt and we made the drive to Pomona Valley Hospital together. We didn't talk on the way. We both knew how serious it was.

The ventilator had been removed and his heartbeat was dropping. We just waited and watched.

Drop.

Drop.

Drop.

Until he was gone.

My relationship with my father was obviously not perfect, but I will be forever grateful for those five years he spent with us, sober, happy, and present. There was a time when I thought I would never let him near me again, but we needed each other. He gave what he could for as long as he could and that gift is something I wouldn't trade for anything in the world.

Family can be tricky, and some of you may think that putting up walls is your only solution, but there are things worth trying that could support you. Professional help like therapy is wonderful because you have an impartial person to help you communicate and to teach you tools for dealing with difficult situations. In most cases, working on yourself by reading, personal development, meditation, and getting a well-developed ego can help you work through it and make all the difference. This can be very delicate, but it is true; if you are not right with your source it will affect all other areas of your life.

As you begin to make these shifts, remember they are not about being "right." This is about living from a place of honesty and using the ideas that have come before this chapter to clear the garden of your life. This may take a good deal of time, as it is probably overgrown from neglect. Just be diligent in clearing up misunderstandings and disagreements promptly, so the garden does not get out of control again. It takes consistent care.

In addition to not insisting on being right, it is important to be present with your source. In human communication, we often aren't listening to other people, just waiting for our turn to talk. Sometimes we even think we are listening, but our mind-chatter, anxieties, and musings can drown out the person who is speaking. Also, we often only hear things that affect us. We listen from a place of self-centeredness where we only hear what has to do with us. There is no way to remain present in this mindset.

For example, when my sister Brenda was living in my guest house and told me she wanted to move out, my first thought was, "She is leaving me." I didn't ask her why. I didn't try to understand. I just saw how it would affect me, and it made me mad. We got into an argument and I wanted to be right, versus remembering who she is to me and why I love her so much. Why would I want to put tears in her eyes? I want the best for her.

Another time, at a family gathering Brenda made my niece cry. I didn't know what had happened, but I flew off the handle and went after her. How dare she make that kid cry? She already had so much to deal with! I knew how to push my sister's buttons and I went for the throat with a loud comment that I knew would hurt her. She came at me, physically attacking me and I defended myself. There was hair pulling and the whole, undignified, unnecessary thing was my fault. I could have done 10 other things that would have had a different result. I was almost 40 years old and I started a fist fight with my sister.

Again, if I had been present and not in my crazy head, I would never have been able to cause a fight with my sister. After it all calmed down, I said, "Hey, I love you. I'm sorry about the miscommunication. I never meant to hurt you." I wanted to make her feel better. I didn't want to be defensive and I didn't care about being right.

One of the other commitments I have made is not to contribute to gossip. Gossip was a big part of my upbringing. Having the inside story was a kind of currency in my neighborhood. Spreading scandal and betraying confidences was a way to prop yourself up while reporting on things that were none of your business and were often not true. In that neighborhood we fought for everything. We fought for food, clothes, money, and also attention. Gossip got you plenty of attention.

We were defensive and it was like life was one big fight. It felt like there was always somebody trying to take something from you. Even intangible things like your honor, your ego, or your reputation. That day with my sister took us back in time to behavior that had been instilled in us for decades. Getting right with my source has been a process, and it has been messy at times and I'm always going to be working on it. The important part is remembering that you choose how to respond. Choose to be positive and ask questions rather than right-fighting.

If we clear up misunderstandings, they will not digress into fist fights or result in cutting off communication for years. Being present and honoring your commitments to yourself and your source take practice. This is true with friendships and in the workplace as well as just being a good member of society. You get to choose how to respond. You choose your input. Choose the best life has to offer. It's all about searching, staying open, giving, receiving, loving, connecting, and growing.

Chapter 22: How Can I Raise the Bar?

"If you're unwilling to leave someplace you've outgrown, you will never reach your full potential. To be the best, you have to constantly be challenging yourself, raising the bar, pushing the limits of what you can do. Don't stand still, leap forward." - Ronda Rousey

Last summer, Elbert and I were in the Jacuzzi after a nice day around the house. We had not done anything exciting, some cleaning around the house, some yard work, and a little time in the pool. It was about 9:00PM. The bubbles from the Jacuzzi felt so good on my back; it was like a massage. We were having this lovely peaceful moment of appreciation for the view and the time we had spent together. Then we started playing this game we love.

"Do you know what would make this even better?" he asked. "If we cut back the hedges so we had even more of the view."

"What would make it even better is if we had some champagne," I replied.

"And some cheese and crackers," he said.

"And someone to bring cheese and crackers to us!" I added.

The idea behind this game is not to complain about what we don't have in the moment, but to play lightly with what else is possible. We love and appreciate what is already there and think about how we could make it even better next time. I call it a game, but it is also a practice in sharing and building something with your partner.

When Elbert and I were planning our trip to Dubai, we knew we wanted to make the visit incredible and raise the bar on the expected. We went to the top floor of the Burj Khalifa, which is the tallest building in the world. In Abu Dhabi we went to a very fancy restaurant where we had little biscuits and coffee with gold flakes in it. All for only $200! Then we went to Ferrari World which is the world's biggest indoor amusement park with the fastest roller coaster in the world. There are plenty of things to see and do there, but our game of raising the bar made it thrilling and decadent.

To raise the bar means to increase your standards or expectations. You create your own measure for the way you want to live your life. I find that my habit of recognizing 10 positive things each day before bed is very helpful. I am grateful that I lived the day, I'm happy that my family is safe and healthy, that I have a comfortable bed to sleep in, etc. I see my growth and my accomplishments and it brings me to the present moment. The more I focus on these things, the more of it I create. At night I also ask God to continue to bless me with good health and abundance so that I can help others and do His work.

Connecting with my faith and recognizing the wonderful life I have helps me get through anything. Appreciate yourself too! No one knows how incredible you are better than you do. Affirming your own awesomeness can open the door to a second date, a new career opportunity, or making a valuable connection with someone else. Maintain awareness of your strengths and talents.

There was a time when I could list all of my shortcomings and all of the things I didn't like about myself. That was my comfort zone then. I was very familiar with all the things I wasn't good at doing. It was also so much of what I heard from people around me. For some people, cutting themselves down is their default setting. Maybe they believe it, maybe they want someone else to boost them up by objecting to their negative self-talk, but it is pervasive and detrimental to us all. It erodes confidence and invites more misery. Notice when you say something negative about yourself and notice when people around you do it. It is insidious and an awful way to live your life!

I replaced all of those kinds of thoughts and comments with the new list of appreciation. I am a loving mother, I'm fun, I'm active, I contribute to others, I have a big heart, I am a good listener, and on and on. I am good at a lot of things. I can't give you the list of things I am not happy about. I don't make that list. It is not part of my world anymore.

This is another area where being clear about what you love and what is important to you comes into play. When I mention in conversation how much I love golf, if the listener happens to love golf too, we can connect. If I am unclear and don't make the effort to connect, we will miss that chance with one another. Once you are clear on what you love, let people know. This creates more possibilities for connection and growth. If you are on a first date and say something like, "I really love and value my family and that's where I like to spend my time," your date may or may not share that value with you, but you will both know right away. You won't have to deal with the crazy annoyance of guessing and waiting to find out where you connect. You can also do this when interviewing for a job by letting the interviewer know what is important to you in the workplace and what you love to do. This is where knowing how awesome you are allows you to shine. This will clear the way for jobs, connections, romantic relationships, and change.

So if you are going to raise the bar in your life, you need to affirm what is already positive and then think about how you could make it even better. If you tell people that you like daisies, chocolates, and jewelry or nice scarves and perfume, then you might get what you want there too. But if you are the only one who knows, how can it appear in your life? Don't keep these things a secret. As you are raising the bar, share it.

Whenever I have a breakthrough or an "aha" moment, I share it with people. Sharing it solidifies it for me even more. As Joseph Joubert said, "To teach is to learn twice over." You can expand your growth even further if you are willing to share your learnings.

This is play and it's very simple, but it must be intentional and practiced to get the most out of it. Before you know it, that bar will be way up beyond where it currently is and your life will be better than ever.

Chapter 23: Always Be Creating

"You can't cross the sea merely by standing and staring at the water." - Rabindranath Tagore

Recently I created a vision for 15 years from now. I will be 61 years old and live in a beach house overlooking the ocean in Santa Barbara. My body will be fit and my hair will be long. I will have satin sheets and sexy satin pajamas. I see it and I know it will happen.

I am always creating and seeing forward. I make a plan and fill in the details. With the plan above, I woke up one day and went to a real estate website and started looking at properties in Santa Barbara just to price it out. Knowing what it will take to get that house gets me so excited! As I have already told you, it is very positive to put an idea out into the world and begin to make it take shape with some small action. I fill in a few details and opportunities seem to flow in.

When my business needed to expand into other parts of California, I had to travel more and more and I needed an easy way to get from place to place. I was looking into helicopter transportation, and an email arrived to my inbox about jet service. I had no idea you could buy a membership and travel in a private jet. I never would have known if I hadn't put the idea out into the world.

(Traveling this way is *wonderful.* You don't have to go to a big airport. You drive right up to a hangar and you give your car to a valet attendant. You can arrive 15 minutes before takeoff. You go through screening when you first subscribe to the service, so you don't have to show I.D. or have your bag examined. We can bring our pets with us into the cabin. The people from the service know you by name. When I return from my travels my car is waiting for me at the front door of the hangar. They have my schedule, so I just get in and go.)

In the last chapter I said that you need to tell people what you want, so that they may just give it to you. This is similar. I was in a group of people talking about an upcoming trip to Las Vegas and I mentioned that I would love to stay in a penthouse at the Aria Resort. An acquaintance in the group told me he gambled at the Aria and they often comped him a penthouse that I could have when I wanted it. Amazing! What if I hadn't said anything? This kind of thing has come up time and time again with tickets to events I have expressed an interest in, people I have wanted to meet, and places I have wanted to visit. I put a little energy into expressing a desire for something and an opportunity pops up.

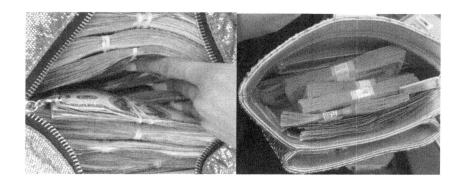

One of my practices is keeping photos of the things I want in my life. I also keep quotes that inspire me. I save pictures on my phone of yachts and cars and luxury items like that. I have lots of pictures of stacks of money. One photo that I love is of a woman's nicely manicured hands over a big handbag full of money. Whenever I am scrolling through my photos (which is very often as I show off my family or something else I love) I see these other photos of the things I want in my life. I attract them. While I was in

Las Vegas (staying in the Aria penthouse, thank you very much) I won a jackpot of a little over $40,000. They gave me my winnings in cash; I had never had that much cash at once in my life! When I looked at the money in my purse, it was almost exactly like the picture on my phone.

You can play with images like this too. It's helpful just to have a reminder of what you are creating and it keeps it fun and light. Keeping the energy easy is important. If you become desperate for something this really doesn't work. (As I heard in a movie once, "Desperation -- it's the world's worst cologne.")

Don't let life just happen to you. Be a participant! If you are not being a partner to the universe in making your world, you'll end up aimlessly floating around like a boat with no rudder to pull you forward in the direction of your dreams. You still might get what you want, but it will be with much more effort and time. So focus on being playful and notice what is showing up in your life. Always be creating the incredible world you deserve and want.

Chapter 24: Call Out the Miracles, Live in the Miracles

"There are only two ways to live your life. One is as though nothing is a miracle. The other is as though everything is a miracle." - Albert Einstein

Each day the world awakens and people set off about their busy lives. The way most of us live is not really a stage set to recognize miracles, but miracles happen around us all the time. When you change your perception of what a miracle is you begin to see them everywhere. Don't walk around like a zombie and miss them!

Driving across town without having a car accident is a miracle. Flying in an airplane across the country in a matter of a few hours is a miracle. Your body's ability to heal itself, to digest food, and to innately feel when something is not right is one of the most incredible miracles. When you are stuck in your story or living Groundhog Day, you will not have the ability to see and appreciate this kind of miracle. You won't notice miraculous happenings and you won't be able to create your own miracles.

When you acknowledge the bounty of miracles in your life, you will create a powerful energy that sparks transformation and possibility. For example, in one of my businesses, Ortega Counseling Center, we assist injured workers in training for new careers. I declared that I wanted 100% of qualifying injured workers in California to get their job loss training benefits. I wanted that miracle to happen, so I called it out. I became an advocate for these injured workers. I took action. I got people behind me to support my efforts and it made all the difference. The law was changed and the miracle I wanted was realized, resulting in the improvement of countless people's lives. They were able to retrain in fields that interested them and make a living doing things they were excited about. That was the miracle I asked for and when it came to fruition I thought I would burst with gratitude!

Look for miracles out in the world. Acknowledge the greatness of the changing of the seasons or the incredible technology that allows us to have a conversation with someone thousands of miles away. Understand that miracles sometimes show up differently than you expected them, but in that lies perfection. If you look at where I began my life, I am really not supposed to be where I am now. I went from holding no value in education to believing in it completely as the miracle that transformed my life and the lives of my children. I went from welfare and bounced checks to abundance, private jets, and financial freedom. I grew up in constant chaos and drama and now I live a peaceful and drama-free life, and I created both.

Throughout this book I have recalled terrible things from my childhood but I can also look back and remember the good things.

Especially in the early days, my mother invested her time and attention in us to a fault. She made sure we were at school, we weren't allowed to date or hang around the neighborhood where all the mischief and madness happened. We hated her for this at the time, but in hindsight, it was the most loving thing she could have done. Being a tough mom is difficult. If she had let us do whatever we wanted and never tracked us down or disciplined us, it may have been easier but she knew that could lead to disaster. She wanted us to succeed and do better than she did. She often talked to us about the worth of a woman. Even though she couldn't see her own worth and value, she instilled it in us with her words of affirmation and the stories she shared of her own life lessons. "Don't be dumb and stay with a man who cheats on you or beats you." "Don't have a lot of children." "You are special, beautiful and can have anyone you want as a husband, even the President of the United States." My mother shaped us to be strong, independent women. I miss her every day, but I know she would be proud to see her children as we are now. We are all in loving relationships based on respect and admiration...a true miracle.

The work that I have done over the years has provided for some pretty amazing miracles. I took my daughter to Paris two years ago. We went to the Eiffel Tower. We went to the Louvre. We visited every iconic place in Paris. We were able to have VIP access, so we saw things that are not open to the general public. We didn't have to wait in any lines. Our host took us right to the front of every attraction and exhibit.

When I took my daughter to the Louis Vuitton store, I told her she could pick out anything that she wanted. She got nervous, and she asked, "What kind of mother does that?" Now she's used to it. She's always asking me for luxury items now, but that trip was our first experience with having no budget to stick to. It was hard for her to believe.

I went to Gandhi's home while we were in India. We learned about his life and saw the exact spot where he was killed. I was in India for a global event for the Entrepreneurs' Organization where the vice president of India, Shri Venkaiah Naidu spoke to us. He arrived in an ambulance only four days after having open-heart surgery. That was hugely impactful on me because I could see that his vision was bigger than he was. It was a miracle.

When we visited Mount Everest, we had to fly into the most dangerous airport in the world. The airport in Nepal has high winds, cloud cover, high terrain, and a 2,000 foot drop at one end of the airport. Landing safely, was a miracle! We had a champagne breakfast at the summit of Mount Everest.

When I went the Taj Mahal, we had a VIP tour. We arrived in time to see the miracle of the sunrise and a horse-drawn carriage carried us through.

The businesses I own are so gratifying. The Ortega Counseling Center helps injured workers create possibilities and find training for new careers. We started with one employee and we now have 33. Another miracle!

I have a restaurant called The Nixon Chops & Whiskey which was recently named one of the Top, Best Restaurants in L.A. according to the L.A. Times and by various magazines. Our chef is known from Bravo's *Top Chef*. He is highly respected and appears on television all the time. It's a really fun, popular spot. I never could have imagined this, it is a miracle!

I have a marketing and advertising company, Asor, named after my mother ("Rosa" spelled backward). I have real estate holdings, properties, rental units, and commercial properties. I also have an investment company which invests in people's ideas, and the designer sensation, Savvy Sox! And there is the non-profit organization called Angels for Injured Workers which assists injured workers and their families who are in need. Most recently I am starting an employment leadership academy.

Does this sound like the life of a girl who grew up in gangland? I have been granted miracles and I have worked miracles with nothing more than the information I have shared with you in the pages of this book.

Now is your time. We all have the capacity to create miracles in our lives. You have everything you need inside of you. The life of your dreams is within your reach. You can do it. Dream big. No! Bigger than that! You are worthy and you are loved. Just do the work, follow the steps, no matter how much of a stretch it seems. Know what you want for yourself. Do the difficult stuff. Touch people and make miracles in the lives of everyone you touch.

Don't wish your life away waiting for some great future moment. Be ready and willing. Make it now. YOU are the miracle worth mastering.

Made in the USA
Monee, IL
08 October 2020

44237520R10115